Azaleas Rhododendrons Camellias

By the Editors of Sunset Books and Sunset Magazine

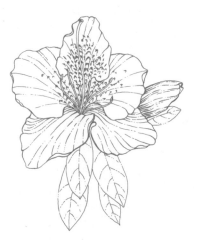

Lane Publishing Co. • Menlo Park, California

Acknowledgments

The beauty and variety of azaleas, rhododendrons, and camellias have long attracted the attention of gardeners, and each plant has acquired a devoted and enthusiastic following, both among general gardeners and among individuals who specialize in the cultivation and development of these plants. This book relies heavily on the collective experience of such plant specialists, who have generously shared knowledge gained from years of experience.

For their assistance in checking information on azaleas and rhododendrons, we appreciate the assistance of Mr. and Mrs. Everett Farwell, Woodside, California; Fred Galle, Pine Mountain, Georgia; Harold Greer, Eugene, Oregon; William Moynier, Los Angeles, California; George Ring, Fairfax, Virginia; E. Parker Smith, Sebastopol, California; and Theodore Van Veen, Portland, Oregon.

For their help with camellias copy, we are indebted to Mr. and Mrs. A. B. Cooper, Nashville, Tennessee; Mr. and Mrs. J. W. Ellis, Keystone Heights, Florida; Edward M. Lewis, Bellevue, Washington; James H. McCoy, Fayetteville, North Carolina; Julius Nuccio, Altadena, California; and Jack Osegueda, Oakland, California.

For assistance in photography, special thanks go to Kathryn Arthurs, Greer Gardens, Huntington Botanical Gardens, Nuccio's Nursery, Van Veen Gardens, and William Woodroof.

Readers who want to learn more about azaleas, rhododendrons, and camellias and meet other enthusiasts may wish to join societies devoted to these plants. For information on the American Rhododendron Society (which covers both rhododendrons and azaleas), write to 14635 S.W. Bull Mt. Road, Tigard, OR 97223. Camellia lovers can request membership information from the American Camellia Society, P.O. Box 1217, Fort Valley, GA 31030. Members of each organization receive quarterly publications and membership in regional and local chapters of the society.

Edited by Philip Edinger

Design: *Joe di Chiarro*
Illustrations: *Linda Gatto,*
Cynthia Bassett

Cover: Congenial garden companions produce a bounty of springtime floral color. Featured at left is venerable **Camellia japonica** 'Kumasaka'; in foreground is Rutherfordiana azalea 'Alaska'; rhododendron hybrid 'Royal Pink' provides a lush pink backdrop. Photographed by Ells Marugg.

Photographers

Jack McDowell: 22 (bottom left). **Ells Marugg:** 17, 18, 19, 20 (top, center left, right), 22 (top, bottom right), 23 (top, bottom right), 49, 50 (bottom left, bottom right), 51 (top left), 52 (bottom left, bottom right), 53 (top left, top right, bottom right), 54, 55 (top right, bottom left, bottom right), 56, 57, 58 (top), 59 (top left, top right, bottom left), 60 (top, bottom right), 61, 62 (top, bottom left), 63, 64, 89, 90, 91, 92, 93, 94, 95 (top left, bottom left, bottom right), 96. **Don Normark:** 21, 23 (bottom left), 51 (bottom), 55 (top left), 58 (bottom), 60 (bottom left), 62 (bottom right). **Norman A. Plate:** 95 (top right). **Michael Thompson:** 20 (bottom left), 24, 50 (top), 51 (top right), 52 (top), 53 (bottom left), 59 (bottom right).

Editor, Sunset Books: David E. Clark

First printing February 1982

Contents

Azaleas   4
Bountiful showoffs to brighten your garden

Rhododendrons   24
Elegant beauties in a rainbow of colors

Camellias   64
A gift from the Orient to the world

Azaleas

The word "azalea" conjures an image of masses of colorful blooms. And that's exactly what azaleas deliver—whether under Southern live oaks draped with Spanish moss, in a Pacific Northwest or east coast woodland garden, or spilling out of a redwood container on a southern California patio. Colors range from delicate to garish, hot to cool, solid to variegated. But whatever effect you want, you can be sure that a healthy azalea will be smothered in blossoms in its season.

What Is an Azalea?

A botanist would tell you that an azalea is classified as a kind of rhododendron; and a close comparison of the flowers and foliage of azaleas and rhododendrons will show why. The box "Azaleas versus Rhododendrons" on page 7 clarifies the relationships.

But from the gardener's viewpoint, azaleas differ enough from most popular rhododendrons to be treated as different plants that just happen to prefer much the same culture (see page 6).

To begin with, there are two main types of azaleas: evergreen and deciduous. The evergreen sorts—typified by the azaleas to be found in florists' shops—are hybrids of species from China, Korea, Taiwan, and Japan. Colors include pinks and reds, orange red, lavender, purple, and white—but not yellow. The deciduous species, more widespread in nature, are found in southern Europe, Japan, and China; one species is native to the west coast of North America, and over half hail from the eastern United States and Canada. Colors include soft and bright tones of yellow, orange, and red; and shades of pink, white, and lavender. Some species and hybrids are notably fragrant. Before the annual autumn leaf drop, many produce a second burst of color from foliage that turns yellow, rusty orange, or autumnal red.

Discovery and Development

The recorded history of azaleas begins around 400 B.C. with an account of Greek soldiers who became dangerously ill after eating honey made from nectar of the Pontic azalea (*Rhododendron luteum*), which was growing where the troops had camped along the Black Sea. Three hundred years later, a Roman army was massacred at almost the same location, the troops having become stupefied after eating honey from the same source.

The entry of azaleas into Western horticultural history began with the English who, while they were building their empire during the 18th and 19th centuries, collected species from their various colonies. By 1800 many native American azaleas (all deciduous) had reached English gardens—enthusiastically sent to the mother country by collectors who explored the territory from New England through the Appalachian Mountains to the southern Gulf Coast. By that time, too, the infamous Pontic azalea was also growing in England.

The East India companies of Great Britain and Holland also imported a number of Asian azaleas (both deciduous and evergreen sorts) to Europe during the 18th and 19th centuries; among them were some Japanese azaleas obtained via China or Indonesia, since Japan was at that time virtually closed to trade with the western world.

By the 1820s many species of both deciduous and evergreen azaleas were available to European horticulturists who eagerly took up the challenge of raising hybrid offspring from deliberate crosses.

Nineteenth century groundwork

In the early years of azalea hybridizing, Belgium led other countries in the production of new varieties—surviving today in the evergreen Belgian Indica hybrids and the deciduous Ghent hybrids. Throughout the 19th century, additional species were sent from the Orient to Britain, Belgium, Holland, and France, and were immediately recruited into hybridizing programs.

As more and more azaleas were collected from the wild, botanists and horticulturists realized that a number of Asian "species" were actually natural hybrids, some were just varying forms of widespread species, and still others were old garden hybrids developed in Japan during its centuries of isolation. Conversely, several American species sent to Europe turned out to be more than one species gathered under a single name. The ancestries of both evergreen and deciduous hybrids are complex, and the confused identity of some parent plants makes it difficult to sort out exact backgrounds of today's hybrids.

In the mid-1800s, the introduction to England of America's western azalea (*Rhododendron occidentale*) added a new dimension to deciduous azalea breeding—one that is noticeable to this day. Combined with the typical yellow, orange, and red hybrids of the Chinese and Japanese deciduous azaleas (and, in some cases, also with Appalachia's flame azalea *R. calendulaceum*), *R. occidentale* produced seedlings that broadened the color range to include soft pink, salmon, cream, and white. It left its imprint on blossom form, too, producing broader petals and blooms with a squared-off appearance—a look readily apparent in today's Knap Hill, Exbury, and similar strains.

Mollis hybrid azalea (deciduous)

Twentieth century refinements

By 1900 all the basic parent species of present deciduous azalea hybrids had been assembled and crossed with one another. Improved hybrids produced since then are still derived from the same species.

Evergreen azaleas, on the other hand, have been infused with the blood of different species during this century. Hybridizers in diverse localities have developed new strains, usually in an effort to produce plants adapted to particular climatic conditions: hotter summers, colder winters, or a drier atmosphere, for example. The various azalea races are described on pages 12–13.

Azaleas in the Landscape

With their cheerful variety of colors, azaleas are familiar to many people—if only as plants bought from the florist for special occasions. But for those whose only exposure to azaleas has been to the usual florist shop sorts, there is a surprise waiting.

Though azaleas can't offer quite the range of plant, foliage, and flower types that rhododendrons do (remember that azaleas constitute only one series in the group of plants called *Rhododendron*; see page 7), they can easily fit into as many landscape situations. In addition to the deciduous azaleas that provide a second season of interest with colorful autumn foliage, there are low-growing evergreen varieties that can serve as ground covers, compact azaleas and ones that are tall and willowy, plants wider than they are tall or the reverse, and some that will attain the size of small trees when mature. With such a variety of raw material, you can plant borders, hedges, barriers, or backdrops of diverse proportions—all of which will blaze with color in season and have a neat appearance during the rest of the year.

Azaleas look at home in plantings near water, and they're also prime subjects for oriental-style gardens because their branch structure can be guided easily into characteristic horizontal planes. Singly or in groups, azaleas in containers (see page 7) will dramatically enhance a patio, terrace, deck, or porch. And like their rhododendron relatives, azaleas are unexcelled as components of lightly shaded woodland gardens.

Basic Azalea Culture

The differences between the "average" evergreen or deciduous azalea and the "typical" large-flowered rhododendron are comparable to the differences among various classes of roses (miniature versus floribunda versus hybrid tea, for example). Plants and blossoms vary in appearance, but their basic cultural needs are the same—with particular types of individuals performing better in certain climates, exposures, and soil types.

In general, then, we can say that azaleas are like rhododendrons in these respects:
• They're forest understory plants, for the most part, preferring good light but protection from strong direct sun and from forceful, drying winds.
• They need a soil that is well drained, moisture retentive, acid, and rich in organic matter.

• They're shallow-rooted, with root systems of many species consisting of a mass of fibrous roots, and thus are easy to transplant.

Carrying the analogy one step further, we can say that the general guidelines regarding garden location, soil preparation, planting, and subsequent care (watering, mulching, fertilizing) for rhododendrons also apply to azaleas. These guidelines are thoroughly explained beginning on page 28.

One important difference between many azaleas and most rhododendrons is that azaleas generally have a greater tolerance for heat. It's the ability of azaleas to perform in humid or fairly dry heat that enables gardeners in the deep South and in central and southern California to grow various evergreen azaleas. Among deciduous sorts, those native to the southeastern United States thrive in that region's humidity and heat—conditions that defeat most named sorts of Exbury, Knap Hill, Mollis, and Ghent hybrids.

Pruning Azaleas

Unlike most rhododendrons, azaleas have growth buds all along their stems, just under the bark surface. As a result, new growth will originate close to any cut you make.

Most evergreen azaleas need little pruning other than removal of weak or dead wood and whatever trimming is required to keep plants shapely or within bounds. If you want a compact plant rather than one that's open and irregular, cut back some of the thicker limbs to a foot or less; the cut branches will put forth strong new shoots to fill in the plant. On the other hand, if you want to emphasize a plant's irregular or picturesque form (many azaleas, both evergreen and deciduous, tend to produce growth in layered tiers that suggest training in the

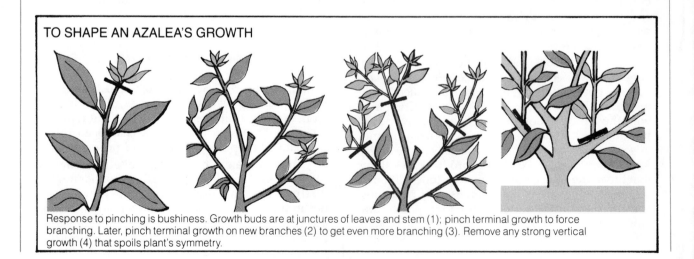

TO SHAPE AN AZALEA'S GROWTH

Response to pinching is bushiness. Growth buds are at junctures of leaves and stem (1); pinch terminal growth to force branching. Later, pinch terminal growth on new branches (2) to get even more branching (3). Remove any strong vertical growth (4) that spoils plant's symmetry.

AZALEAS VERSUS RHODODENDRONS

Properly, all azaleas are rhododendrons. Even a casual look at azaleas and rhododendrons will reveal obvious similarities. But in the early years of modern plant classification—beginning in 1753 with the publication of Linnaeus' *Species Plantarum*—azaleas and rhododendrons were established as separate genera. So there are some significant differences as well.

The extensive plant collecting done in Asia during the late 19th and early 20th centuries revealed the great range of the genus *Rhododendron* (upward of 900 species) and the great variation in appearance among these plants: from heathlike ground covers to tropical-looking trees. Despite the botanical affinities of all the rhododendrons, amateurs and botanists alike realized the need to classify the species in a way that would acknowledge the underlying relationship but categorize the various differences among them.

Until recently, the most widely used system was the one devised by Sir Isaac Bayley Balfour. He divided the genus *Rhododendron* into a number of *series*, each of which contained from one to several species that appeared to be closely related. With few exceptions, each series was named for one of its prominent species; and if a series contained many species, it was further divided into smaller, more closely knit *subseries*.

One series that does not bear the name of a prominent species is the series *Azalea*. Grouped in their own series are all the "special" rhododendrons that the gardening public knows as azaleas.

Today the original series system is being revamped according to contemporary research that is realigning some of the species' affinities. But the basic series concept still provides an organizational framework that will accommodate future adjustments and additions.

oriental style), just remove stems that interfere with the desired effect, cutting them back to their points of origin on other branches.

Certain deciduous azaleas (Knap Hill, Ghent, and Mollis hybrids) will remain youthful and productive if you periodically remove old declining wood. At any indication of reduced vigor, cut the weakening stem to the ground; new growth will soon replace it.

The best time of year to undertake any pruning or trimming is right after plants have flowered. New growth formed after such pruning will likely bear flower buds for the next year's bloom. Pruning after midsummer will cut down on the number of blossoms the following year since flower buds begin forming at that time.

Azaleas in Containers

Many azaleas, especially the evergreen sorts, are naturals for growing in containers—a fact demonstrated by the hundreds of thousands of container-grown azaleas sold by florists each year. Consider the following reasons for raising some container azaleas of your own.

Landscape flexibility. If you intend to grow azaleas just for the impact of their floral display, you can have instant deck or patio decorations with blooming azaleas in tubs or pots. You can even maintain your own flower show for several months by growing a selection of varieties that come into bloom at overlapping intervals during the flowering season; you can carry waning performers off-stage to a shady garden area or lath house and replace them with a container of another variety just coming into full flower.

Mobility is the major point in favor of growing azaleas in containers. Should you discover that a plant is receiving too much (or too little) sun, is vulnerable to the wind or winter chill, or just doesn't look as good as you had thought it would in its location—you can simply move it, without any of the effort of digging and replanting.

Cultural advantage. In some marginal portions of azalea country, a container-grown plant may be the solution to the factors that make the area marginal and therefore risky. Hot, dry summers, alkaline soil or water, and poorly drained soil are three inhospitable influences that may be circumvented with a container environment.

Native azaleas—all decidious species—grow in many parts of the United States and Canada. *Rhododendron occidentale* ranges from southern California into Oregon. In the eastern part of the continent, species can be found in their own particular areas from steamy Florida to Labrador. They're especially abundant from the Atlantic coast westward through the Appalachian Mountains and down through the deep South to the Gulf coast. Texas, Oklahoma, Arkansas, and Missouri also claim native species.

Evergreen azaleas (as well as some decidious species) hail from eastern Asia—China to Japan. They and their hybrids have proven adaptable to the Pacific coast, southern states, and Atlantic seaboard as far north as their winter cold tolerances will allow.

What, then, is "Azalea Country?" It depends on what azaleas you want to grow and how much special attention, in less favorable regions, you're willing to give them. For outdoor culture in the ground, the evergreen sorts are largely restricted to areas without severe winter cold; how much cold they'll endure depends on their ancestry (see page 12). Deciduous sorts extend the boundaries of "Azalea Country" into the chilly-winter northern states and the midwestern heartland, where low temperatures can dip to −25 or −30°F/−32 or −35°C. Where the map is unshaded—from the western plains states through the Rocky Mountains and on through the Great Basin and Sonoran deserts—dry atmosphere and alkaline soil combined with either extreme winter cold or intense summer heat rule out azaleas' success or even survival.

Highlighting the unusual. A number of evergreen azaleas can be trained to cascade over the edge of a container—just right for display in hanging baskets or trailing over the face of a wall (see photograph on page 23). And plants that have been trained into tree form or that have been carefully pruned in oriental style can be especially striking when featured in a container for close-up viewing.

Container culture

On a plant growing in a container, roots are restricted to making the best of whatever materials you've provided for them. There's never the modifying influence, found in the garden, of surrounding soil that can affect acidity, moisture content, even soil texture in the immediate root area. The type of growing medium you give your container plant will determine its ability to assimilate water and fertilizers—in short, to thrive.

Soil preparation. Just as in preparing garden soil for azaleas, the emphasis in container soil preparation is on making soil that is porous but nevertheless retains moisture well.

The most satisfactory container soil mixes contain about 75 percent organic matter—occasionally more, but never less than 50 percent of the total volume. Components may vary, but a typical good combination is 50 percent peat moss, 25 percent leaf mold, 25 percent sharp sand (builder's sand) or perlite. This mixture combines good moisture retention, acid reaction, and sharp drainage. You may reduce the proportions of peat and sand and add ground bark (pine, fir, or redwood); bark retains some moisture but drains well. If your garden soil is sandy to sandy loam, you can use it—but never to exceed 20 percent of the total mixture; the remaining 80 percent of the total should consist entirely of organic materials.

Gardeners in the East and South, where summer rainfall combines with hot, humid weather, need to pay special attention to the aeration of a container soil mixture. Where summers are hot and humid, rhododendrons especially and some azaleas are sensitive to excess soil moisture and are more subject to rhododendron wilt fungus, which thrives in warm, damp soil. In such regions a container soil mixture should contain coarse-textured material to increase the air space within the mixture. Bark chips make a good, coarse-textured organic additive, and can be used to make up to 20 percent of the mixture's total volume.

Watering. Attention to watering is your greatest responsibility to a container-grown azalea. Roots should never dry out, but they should not remain saturated either. How often you should water will depend on the exact container soil mixture—how moisture-retentive it is—on the type of container, and on weather conditions.

With any container-grown plant, you may encounter a gradual buildup of harmful salts in the planting mix. Such an accumulation may stem from salts in your water or from fertilizers, or both, and may manifest itself as a white deposit on the soil surface or as plant damage: chlorosis, marginal leaf burn, and even defoliation are common symptoms to watch for.

To avoid salt damage, always water container plants thoroughly so that water runs freely out the bottom of the container. A periodic flushing of container soil mix will go far toward minimizing or eliminating any salt buildup. Every month, if your water supply is alkaline or has a high mineral salt content, fill the container with water several times until water flows out of the drainage hole for several minutes; once every 3 months is sufficient where water quality is good.

Fertilizing. Planted in a well-drained mixture and subjected to frequent, thorough waterings, a container-grown azalea will need periodic nutrient applications.

There are a number of fertilizers, both granular and liquid, that are made especially for acid-loving plants in general or for rhododendrons and azaleas in particular. Any of these will be satisfactory for your container plants, provided they contain nitrogen in the ammonium form and are used according to directions. See page 35 for a discussion of the various types of fertilizers and how and when to use them.

Pest and Disease Control

Rare is the popular garden plant that will not be visited occasionally by one or more of the common garden pests or diseases (aphids and mildew, for example); many garden favorites may also play host now and then to pests or diseases that are specific to a particular plant. Azaleas are no exception—but note our use of the words "occasionally" and "now and then."

An enumeration of potential pests and diseases should be regarded as a source of information, not a suggestion of impending disaster. A number of problems are limited to certain regions or can occur only when weather conditions favor them. Refer to page 39 in the chapter on rhododendrons for a discussion of the various environmentally caused problems and then to page 10 for information on potential pests, diseases, their symptoms, and control measures. Those that may also affect azaleas are indicated by an asterisk (*).

AZALEA AND RHODODENDRON PESTS AND DISEASES

Problem	Symptom	Where Found	Control
Pests:			
Weevils*	Adults chew leaf edges, grubs in soil feed on roots. Affected plants wilt more than others during warm weather.	Everywhere	Drench soil with diazinon or orthene to kill grubs; spray same material on foliage to kill adults.
Leaf miner	Small caterpillars mine tunnels and patches in leaves, then fold back edges of leaf ends to pupate.	Pacific states, South	Spray foliage with malathion or diazinon, or hand-pick.
Stem borer	Tips of new growth dead or dying in summer or early fall. Following year, grub bores down stem, killing it.	Eastern United States	Cut out and destroy dead or dying growth.
Lacewing fly, White fly*	Mottled leaf surface; undersides of leaves conceal flies and larvae or have dark, varnishlike spots where nymphs hatch.	Eastern states and Pacific Northwest	Spray foliage with cygon, meta-systox-R, or orthene twice at 10-day interval.
Spider mites*	White stippling on leaf surface, dried or burned appearance as damage increases; webbing on leaf undersurface.	Everywhere	Spray foliage with kelthane or orthene twice at 7-day interval.
Scale*	Small cottony white scales on stems, leaf bases, and leaf undersides.	Everywhere	Spray foliage and stems with malathion, diazinon, or orthene.
Diseases:			
Leaf gall*	New growth is malformed—thick and fleshy. More troublesome in wet seasons.	Everywhere	Hand-pick galled foliage. Spray new growth two or three times at 3-week intervals with captan or zineb.
Leaf spot	Leaves have purplish black spots or yellowish spots with brown centers.	Everywhere	Spray foliage with benomyl.
Phytophthora blight	Leaves have water soaked lesions that become brown or silver spotted; brown cankers form on new growth, which then wilts.	Anywhere that humidity is high	Spray foliage with zineb or ferbam twice at 2-week interval.
Petal blight*	Brown or watery spots on petals spreading over entire flower, which soon becomes brown and slimy.	Southeastern United States to California	Drench soil before bloom with terrachlor solution; spray flowers twice a week with thiram or zineb.
Botrytis petal blight	Gray brown mold on petals; flowers not slimy.	Humid climates: East, South, Pacific Northwest	Spray flowers with zineb or benomyl twice a week.
Wilt (Phytophthora, Pythium)	Plant wilted in early morning of a cloudy day; leaves are dull olive green; brown discoloration of wood beneath bark.	Anywhere in over-moist soil	Raise plant or replant in well-drained location; drench root ball, soil with truban.
Damping off	Same symptoms as wilt but without brown discoloration beneath bark.	Anywhere in over-moist soil	Decrease water, improve drainage (see above); drench soil with benlate or thiram.

*affects azaleas as well as rhododendrons

Chlorosis

Soil acidity is measured in *pH* units. A *pH* of 7 is neutral—neither acid nor alkaline; readings above 7 are alkaline, below 7 are acid. The degree of alkalinity/acidity increases or decreases by 10 times the previous level for each whole-number change in the *pH*. Thus, *pH* 8 is 10 times more alkaline than *pH* 7 and 100 times more alkaline than *pH* 6.

Ordinarily, rhododendrons and azaleas prosper in soils between *pH* 4 and 6. Recent research has disclosed, however, that acid soil is not always directly responsible for the good health of these plants: the acidity of the plants' cell sap is the critical factor. Internal acidity guarantees the availability of iron within the plants' tissues; iron is essential to the production of chlorophyll, which in turn manufactures carbohydrates in the leaves and is responsible for the green color. If iron is unavailable to the plant tissues, chlorosis develops; leaf veins remain green while the leaves themselves turn yellow to white. This condition is not unlike anemia in humans and, unless corrected, can be fatal.

Loss of internal acidity can come about in several ways. The most common cause, of course, is alkaline soil—which may also be augmented by alkaline water. For a discussion of this problem and how you can combat it, see page 11.

Another possible cause of chlorosis is an inability of the roots to absorb enough iron for the plant's needs. If you plant rhododendrons too deep, their roots are unable to function efficiently until brought close to the surface—either by the plant's growing new roots in that direction or by your raising the plant. Meanwhile, the plant's health suffers.

Overwatering and overfertilizing can kill so many roots that the remaining ones supply inadequate amounts of iron for the amount of top growth. Roots can also be destroyed, with the same consequences, by various weevil larvae, centipedes, and nematodes.

What to do for a chlorotic plant. Applications of chelated iron in a foliage spray will tell you within a week or two whether chlorosis has resulted from a lack of available iron in a plant's cell sap. Within that time, the iron-deficient leaves will begin to show green spots which will become larger until—in 5 to 6 weeks—the leaves are entirely green again.

Chlorotic symptoms can also reflect a lack of elements other than iron. Magnesium deficiency can be diagnosed by spraying foliage with magnesium sulfate (Epsom salts)—2 tablespoons per gallon of water. If leaves regain their green color, you can obtain a longer-lasting remedy by broadcasting magnesium sulfate crystals on the soil at the rate of 1 pound for each 100 square feet.

If a foliage spray of iron chelates or magnesium sulfate fails to bring about a shift back toward green, you might apply fritted trace elements (FTE) to the soil. These elements are released slowly but over a long period and can be valuable where chlorosis is not the result of a damaged root system.

Although iron chelates in a foliage spray or in soil applications will provide iron to plants for as long as you wish to use it, you'll generally be doing your plants better service if you determine the cause of chlorosis and then apply an appropriate remedy (see also "Alkaline water and soil," below). Especially in areas of alkaline soil, other elements besides iron are likely to become unavailable as the pH increases, requiring remedies in addition to iron chelates.

Whenever chlorosis persists despite your efforts to overcome it and where there is no evidence of root damage, the best course of action is to have your soil analyzed by a state or university agricultural extension service or a professional soil testing laboratory.

Alkaline water and soil

In many areas of the semiarid Southwest, West, and Pacific Northwest (east of the Cascade Mountains) where it's possible to grow some azaleas and rhododendrons, gardeners must work around the handicap of alkaline water and soil. Soils in such low-rainfall regions characteristically contain high concentrations of calcium and magnesium salts; this results in pH readings (see under "Chlorosis" on page 10) of 8.0 or higher. Domestic water in many of these areas is also alkaline, carrying varying amounts of dissolved salts of calcium, magnesium, and other basic elements.

In the East and South, rainfall usually accounts for most or even all of the necessary summer watering; rain regularly waters and leaches the soil with somewhat acidic water. But in the semiarid western regions, most summer water is supplied by irrigation rather than rainfall. Ordinary garden watering may wet the soil to a depth of a foot or so; part of the water is absorbed by plant roots, the rest evaporates from the surface of the soil. As a result, constant irrigation of already alkaline upper soil layers with water carrying alkaline salts leaves a residue of salts and gradually raises the alkalinity and concentration of potentially harmful salts.

Symptoms and remedies. Signs of trouble from alkaline soil or water are chlorosis and leaf burn. Chlorosis is discussed beginning on page 10, and leaf burn is presented under "Windburn and salts injury" on page 39.

Under the "Chlorosis" heading we suggest several corrective measures that can be effective in remedying chlorosis, though they don't affect the soil's alkalinity. Leaching the soil and applying sulfur are additional remedial measures that gardeners in alkaline-soil regions may try.

More than irrigation, leaching is a deliberate flooding of the soil for several hours at a time. Even though the water used in flooding will contain small amounts of dissolved salts, it will pick up some of the salt residue in the soil—the results of months of regular garden watering—and carry it down into the lower soil levels below the range of many plants' roots. One heavy midsummer leaching plus the normal leaching action of winter rains may be all that is needed to keep salt accumulation in check.

For leaching to be effective, your soil must be well drained so that dissolved salts can be carried into lower soil levels. If soil is poorly drained and you have an alkalinity problem, your best chance for success with azaleas or rhododendrons is to grow them in raised beds or containers from which salts can be leached easily and often enough to forestall any problem (see pages 7 and 32).

The leaching attack on salinity affects soil fertility, since leaching will carry off soluble plant nutrients along with the alkaline salts. After leaching, give plants a mild application of soluble fertilizer (liquid or dry); or use one of the organic fertilizers that releases nutrients slowly in your regular feeding program.

Another approach to reducing alkalinity is to apply sulfur—as soil sulfur or iron sulfate—to the soil. Sulfur is most effective on high-calcium alkaline soils in which it combines with the calcium in insoluble compounds to form soluble calcium sulfate; this leaches down into lower soil layers.

Sulfur's chief value is in soils where excess calcium is a problem; where it's not, sulfur's action is simply to increase soil acidity.

The best advice on what material is use and how to use it will come from sources familiar with local soils and water. Consult your state or university agricultural extension service or a professional soil testing laboratory.

AZALEA SHOPPING GUIDE

The following 5 pages contain descriptions of 79 evergreen azaleas and 36 deciduous ones. Nothing like a comprehensive catalog, especially of the evergreen sorts, the listings do cover the varieties most likely to be found in nurseries. Many other varieties may be available in some areas.

Evergreen azalea hybrids

Hybridizers have worked with evergreen azaleas for over 150 years. The usual objective for each hybridizer was to produce a group of plants that would perform well in a particular situation: in the greenhouse, in cold-winter climates, or in hot-summer territory. As a result, many evergreen azalea hybrids sold today can be separated into reasonably distinct groups whose varieties have similar climatic tolerances and often similar growth and flower types.

Listed here are descriptions of the principal evergreen types, each with the code abbreviation used in the chart listings on pages 14–16.

BI—Belgian Indica. This group of hybrids was developed primarily for greenhouse growing, but in mild regions where the lowest temperatures don't fall below 20°F/–6°C, they may also serve as landscape plants. Their evergreen foliage is lush and full, and the large double or semi-double flowers are profuse during the flowering season.

SI—Southern Indica. These are the garden azaleas famous throughout the deep South. Originally they were selections from the Belgian Indicas of varieties that were more rugged and better able to perform in full sun than most other azaleas. Somewhat hardier than Belgian Indicas, they will take temperatures from 10° to 20°F/–12° to –6°C, although some will split bark at 20°F/–6°C and most white-flowered varieties will suffer frozen buds at 20°F/–6°C.

In general, the Southern Indicas grow faster, more vigorously, and taller than other azalea types. You may find them sold as "sun azaleas."

K—Kurume. Garden favorites in Japan for over a century, these plants were developed there for outdoor culture. They grow rather compactly and are densely covered with small leaves. Although the flowers are small, they come out in masses, often in attractive tiers that suggest the plants in Japanese prints.

Kurume azaleas will take temperatures down to 5°F/–15°C and grow well outdoors in half sun, but they cannot endure hot, dry summer winds.

G—Gable. These hybrids were developed in southeastern Pennsylvania as evergreen azaleas of the Kurume type that would take 0°F/–18°C temperatures. Since *R. kaempferi* is an ancestor of all, the Gable hybrids are really a special group of Kaempferi hybrids.

In temperatures at the low range of their tolerance, these plants may lose some foliage. Bloom is heavy from April through May.

GL—Glen Dale. The Glen Dale hybrids take their name from the site of the U.S. Division of Plant Exploration and Introduction station in Maryland. They were developed to get the color and flower size of the southern azaleas on plants that would be hardy in the mid-Atlantic states. Some grow tall and rangy, others low and compact; some have small leaves like the Kurumes, others have large leaves.

Growth rates vary from rapid to slow. These hybrids grow well in half sun, and some varieties will take full sun. During cold winters some leaves will drop. Further developments from the Glen Dales, Back Acres hybrids were created at Pass Christian, Mississippi, to perform well in that part of the South.

M—Macrantha. This group includes plants and are sometimes referred to as Gumpo, Chugai, and Satsuki hybrids. They are hardy to around 5°F/–15°C and include low-growing and dwarf varieties. All of these hybrids are late bloomers, flowering well into June, with flowers larger than those of the Kurumes.

P—Pericat. This is a series of azaleas developed in Pennsylvania for greenhouse forcing. Possibly hybrids of Belgian Indica and Kurume varieties, they look much like the Kurumes and are about as hardy.

R—Rutherfordiana. These hybrids, the American equivalents of the Belgian Indicas, were developed for greenhouse forcing. Like the Belgian Indicas, they are good landscape subjects where temperatures don't go below 20°F/–6°C.

Plants are bushy, in the 2 to 4-foot-high range, with handsome foliage. Flower size is intermediate, between the Belgian Indicas and Kurumes; blossoms may be single, semi-double, or double.

Br, GC, and N—Brooks, Gold Cup, and Nuccio. These three hybrid groups were developed in California and are hardy to about 20°F/–6°C. The Brooks hybrids, from the state's central valley, were developed to tolerate the hot, dry summer climate there. The Gold Cup hybrids combine the large flowers of Belgian Indicas with the vigor of the Rutherfordianas. The Nuccio hybrids are of a mixed ancestry that includes Belgian Indicas and Kurumes; they're especially well adapted to the mild and dry climate of southern California.

Ka—Kaempferi. This is a group of hybrids developed in part from *Rhododendron kaempferi,* similar to the Kurumes but taller and of more open growth. Plants are hardy to –15°F/–26°C but are nearly deciduous in the coldest winters. Flowers are profuse in early spring. Varieties sold as Vuykiana hybrids also come under the Kaempferi heading; and all Gable hybrids, as mentioned at left, are *R. kaempferi* derivatives.

AZALEA FLOWER FORMS

A typical azalea flower has five petals joined at the base to form a tube, giving the flower a trumpet or funnel shape. At the base of the trumpet or funnel, there is also an outer ring of very small green sepals that are joined together like a collar. In the center of the flower are five stamens—sometimes more, but in multiples of five. This arrangement constitutes a *single* flower.

In many cases the filaments of the stamens become petal-like; then you have a *semi-double* or *double* flower, depending on the number of stamens that have a petal-like form.

The term *hose-in-hose* means that the outer ring of normally small green sepals become large, petal-like, and showy. Because they're joined into a tube at the base (like the petals), the actual flower appears to be inside another. In this case the stamen filaments may also become petal-like; then you have a flower that is *semi-double hose-in-hose* or *double hose-in-hose.*

Single   Semi-double   Double

Single hose-in-hose   Semi-double hose-in-hose   Double hose-in-hose

Deciduous azalea hybrids

Development of these hybrids began during the 1820s in Belgium and, as with the evergreen azaleas, has diverged into several hybrid groups. The differences among these hybrid groups, though, are less distinct than among the evergreen types, because all deciduous hybrid groups have some parent species in common.

Eight species were used in various combinations to produce the deciduous hybrids. The American species used were *Rhododendrons calendulaceum, nudiflorum, viscosum, occidentale,* and *arborescens.* China contributed *R. molle,* Japan gave *R. japonicum,* and Eurasia contributed the notorious Pontic azalea *R. luteum.*

The first to emerge were the Ghent hybrids, followed by the Mollis and Occidentale hybrids—all produced before 1900. Currently there is great interest in the Knap Hill hybrids, which originated around 1870. These hybrids feature open, squarish flowers (a contribution of *R. occidentale*) in white, cream, brilliant yellow, orange, red, and all shades of pink. Breeding stock from Knap Hill varieties have given rise to various strains, of which Rothschild's Exbury strain is currently the most prominent.

Other hybridizers working with Knap Hill parent material have called the resulting seedlings by other names (for example, the Ilam hybrids from New Zealand) or simply designated the seedlings as their own "Knap Hill hybrids."

Kn and Ex—Knap Hill and Exbury. These have the largest flowers found on deciduous azaleas (up to 5 inches across) and are hardy to about −20°F/−29°C.

Mo—Mollis. These are upright plants, 4 to 5 feet tall; flowers are 2½ to 4 inches wide in clusters of 7 to 13, in yellow through bright red.

Gh—Ghent. The hardiest of azaleas, many of these have survived −25°F/−32°C. Flowers are yellow to red and pink shades, generally smaller than those of the Mollis hybrids. Upright plants grow 4 to 6 feet tall.

Oc—Occidentale. These are derived from Mollis hybrids and *R. occidentale* from the Pacific states of the U.S. Colors range from white flushed pink and yellow to red with orange markings. Blossoms are the size of those of the Mollis hybrids, but plants range up to 8 feet tall.

In particular, Knap Hill, Exbury, and Mollis hybrids are frequently sold as unnamed and even unbloomed seedlings. These are usually very satisfactory landscape plants because the quality of the hybrid strains is high. But for guaranteed fine flowers, your best bet is to purchase a named hybrid.

All deciduous azaleas need a year or more following planting or moving to reestablish themselves and resume their full blooming vigor.

EVERGREEN AZALEAS (White)

Name	Type	Season of Bloom	Characteristics
Alaska	R	October–April	White flower with chartreuse blotch. Most blooms are semi-double but some may be single or double.
Everest	GL	May	Blossoms are white with chartreuse blotch.
Fielder's White	Sl	February–May	Frilled single white flowers are lightly blotched with chartreuse.
Glacier	GL	March–April	Large shining white single flowers; glossy leaves.
Gumpo	M	May–June	Large single white flowers; low, dense plant.
Helen Close	GL	April–May	Large white flower has pale yellow blotch; small dark leaves on a compact, twiggy plant.
Madonna	Br	February–April	Double white flowers; rapid, bushy growth with plenty of foliage.
Nuccio's Dream Clouds	N	February–April	Ruffled green-throated white flowers are double hose-in-hose. Will grow in sun.
Nuccio's Masterpiece	N	February–April	Very large ruffled white double blossoms. Very vigorous plant with large foliage.
Palestrina	K	March–May	Single blossoms are white with light chartreuse blotch; upright plant.
Perle de Swynaerde	Bl	October–April	Large double white blossoms displayed against deep green foliage.
Purity	R	January–March	Pure white flowers are single to semi-double, hose-in-hose.
Rose Greeley	G	February–May	Fragrant single hose-in-hose flowers are white with chartreuse blotch.
Snow	K	March–April	White hose-in-hose flowers; dead blooms hang on. Upright growth.
Sun Valley	GC	March–May	Large hose-in-hose blossoms are shiny white with green throats.
White April	Sl	February–March	Large single white flowers on an upright plant.
White Gish	R	February–April	White sport of red Dorothy Gish; hose-in-hose flowers on a compact plant with shiny foliage.

EVERGREEN AZALEAS (Lavender to Violet)

Name	Type	Season of Bloom	Characteristics
Constance	R	March–April	Large single frilled lavender pink flowers; light green leaves.
Formosa	Sl	March–April	Fluorescent large single lavender magenta flowers; vigorous, rangy plant. More cold-tolerant than most other Southern Indicas. Synonyms: Coccinea, Phoenicia, Vanessa.
L.J. Bobbink	R	March–April	Fragrant orchid lavender blooms are large and semi-double.
Purple Splendor	G	March–April	Frilled red violet flowers with darker blotch, single and hose-in-hose. Plant is low to medium high, spreading. Purple Splendor Compacta is a more compact plant with smaller leaves.
Sherwood Orchid	K	March–April	Large single flowers are orchid lavender with darker blotches; spreading, medium high plant.
Shinnyo-No-Tsuki	M	April–May	Large single flowers are violet red with white centers.
Violacea	Bl	February–April	Large double rich violet purple flowers. Loose plant needs pinching for best shape.

EVERGREEN AZALEAS (Pink)

Name	Type	Season of Bloom	Characteristics
Anchorite	GL	April	Medium-size rose pink single flowers have an undertone of orange.
Aphrodite	GL	March	Soft rose pink single flowers on a spreading plant with dark foliage.
Avenir	Bl	October–April	Coppery pink double blossoms. Leaves are large and rounded.
Balsaminaeflorum	M	April–May	Small deep salmon pink double flowers look like opening roses; dense plant is low and spreading. A double form of *Rhododendron indicum*. Synonym: Rosaeflora.
Caroline Gable	G	March–April	Shocking pink hose-in-hose blossoms; medium tall plant.
Coral Bells	K	March–May	Small hose-in-hose flowers are coral pink shaded darker in centers; small leaves.
Duc de Rohan	Sl	March–May	Single flowers are salmon with rose throats; spreading plant.
Elegans Superba	Sl	March–May	Watermelon pink medium-size single flowers; tall plant. Synonym: Pride of Mobile.
Fedora	Ka	March–April	Large single flowers are deep rose to salmon pink.
George Lindley Taber	Sl	March–May	Single flowers are large, light pink with darker centers. More cold-tolerant than most other Southern Indicas.
Gumpo Pink	M	May–June	Single rose pink flowers with deeper flecks; low, dense plant. A sport of the white-flowered Gumpo.

Name	Type	Season of Bloom	Characteristics
Hi-Gasa	M	May–June	Very large single blossoms are deepest rose pink with dark-spotted throats.
Jean Haerens	BI	February–May	Large double deep rose pink flowers.
Louise Gable	G	April–May	Flowers are semi-double, salmon pink with darker blotch; plant is low and spreading.
Nuccio's Melody Lane	N	January–May	Large single blossoms are blush pink with rosy red spots in throat; vigorous, upright plant.
Nuccio's Pink Bubbles	N	February–April	Large double light pink flowers; leaves are large and dark.
Nuccio's Polka	N	March–May	Single deep salmon flowers on a compact plant that blooms intermittently over many months.
Paul Schaeme	BI	October–April	Large double salmon pink flowers.
Pink Pearl	K	October–April	Soft pink large double blossoms; upright plant.
Rosebud	G	March–April	Small double hose-in-hose blossoms resemble miniature roses. Very low and compact plant.
Rose Queen	R	February–April	Double deep rose pink flowers have slight fragrance.
Southern Charm	SI	February–April	Large single watermelon pink flowers. Plant is open and spreading, with very large leaves. A sport of Formosa.
Sweetheart Supreme	P	February–March	Small semi-double hose-in-hose flowers are blush pink with darker centers. About as hardy as Belgian Indica types.

EVERGREEN AZALEAS (Red and Orange)

Name	Type	Season of Bloom	Characteristics
Buccaneer	GL	April–May	Brilliant orange red single flowers with darker shadings; plant is upright and spreading.
Campfire	G	May	Hose-in-hose flowers are flame red with darker blotches; dense, upright plant with dark green foliage.
Chimes	BI	October–April	Rich red semi-double bell-shaped blossoms.
Dorothy Gish	R	February–April	Brick red hose-in-hose flowers; compact plant with dark glossy leaves.
Firelight	R	February–April	Bright cherry red hose-in-hose blossoms.
Flame Creeper	M	April–May	Striking scarlet orange single flowers; plant is low and spreading with small leaves.
Glamour	GL	April–May	Large brilliant rose red single flowers; narrow dark green leaves turn bronze in autumn.
Glory of Sunninghill	SI	April–May	Vivid orange red single flowers.
Hexe	K	March–May	Crimson red single hose-in-hose flowers on a fairly low, spreading plant.
Hino-Crimson	K	February–April	Small brilliant red single flowers cover a low to medium high plant; foliage turns red in winter. A sport of Hinodegiri.
Hinodegiri	K	February–April	Cherry red single flowers obscure foliage; branches are carried in tiered layers. Same habit and winter color as Hino-Crimson.
Mme. Alfred Sanders	BI	October–May	Large rich red double flowers on a compact plant.
Nuccio's Sunburst	N	February–April	Semi-double blossoms are bright orange red; very compact plant with small dark foliage.
Orange Sanders	BI	October–May	A sport of Mme. Alfred Sanders, identical except for the orange flowers.
Pride of Dorking	SI	March–April	Brilliant carmine red single flowers; upright, compact plant.
Prince of Wales	SI	February–April	Rose red single or semi-double flowers; upright plant.
Red Poppy	BI	October–May	Very large single to semi-double blossoms are dark red.
Redwing	P	February–April	Bright red ruffled hose-in-hose blossoms; loose plant.
Sherwood Red	K	February–April	Brilliant orange red single flowers; plant drops leaves in coldest weather within its hardiness limits.
Vuyk's Scarlet	K	February–April	Large single flowers in bright scarlet red; compact plant.
Ward's Ruby	K	February–April	Brilliant dark red small single flowers cover a low to medium high, spreading plant. Synonym: Ruby Glow.

EVERGREEN AZALEAS (Variegated)

Name	Type	Season of Bloom	Characteristics
Albert and Elizabeth	BI	October–May	Double flowers are white with salmon pink edges.
Bunkwa	M	May	Single flowers are pale pink to white edged in dark salmon pink.
California Sunset	BI	October–April	Single blossoms are salmon pink edged in white.
Easter Parade	GC	February–April	Ruffled flowers are large, hose-in-hose, pink with white mottling.

Evergreen Azaleas, variegated (cont'd.)

Name	Type	Season of Bloom	Characteristics
Eric Schaeme	Bl	February–March	Double salmon pink flowers have white petal edges.
Geisha	GL	February–March	Single flowers are white speckled and striped pink to red.
Iveryana	Sl	April–May	Large white blossoms are striped with light pink. Low, compact plant.
Mardi Gras	GL	April–May	Very large single flowers are red with petals edged in white.
Nuccio's Harvest Moon	N	February–April	Medium-size single flowers vary from salmon pink to salmon with white centers.
Tickled Pink	R	March–April	Single flowers are salmon rose with white edges.
White Orchids	GC	March–April	Large flowers are single to semi-double, ruffled, white with red throats.

DECIDUOUS AZALEAS

Name	Type	Season of Bloom	Characteristics
Adrian Koster	Mo	Late April	Deep pure yellow 4-inch star-shaped flowers.
Balzac	Ex	Late May	Fragrant star-shaped orange red blooms; 12 to 14 to a truss.
Beaulieu	Ex	Late May	Deep pink buds open to soft pink flowers with orange blotch on upper petal.
Berryrose	Ex	May	Fragrant pale pink flowers with orange centers. New leaves are hairy and bronze-tinted.
Brazil	Ex	Early May	Flowers of bright tangerine red with frilled edges. Relatively small blooms, but in profusion.
Cecile	Ex	May–early June	Deep pink buds opening salmon pink with a yellow blotch. Up to 12 flowers in a truss. Good fall foliage.
Christopher Wren	Mo	Late May	Large chrome yellow flowers with tangerine blotch.
Coccinea Speciosa	Gh	Early June	Flowers are orange with a yellowish orange blotch.
Dr. Jacobi	Mo	Early June	Deep red 4½-inch flowers.
Fireball	Kn	May–early June	Unusually deep red small flowers and bronze green foliage.
Flamingo	Kn	Late April–May	Frilled flamingo pink flowers on a strong plant.
George Reynolds	Ex	April	Large flowers of butter yellow with deep gold blotches, green throats.
Gibraltar	Ex	Early May	Big flowers with ruffled edges; deep orange flushed with red. Compact shrub.
Ginger	Ex	May	Round tight trusses of small bright tangerine flowers.
Golden Dream	Ex	Early June	Golden yellow flowers with orange blotches. Rounded compact clusters of 9 to 11 flowers.
Golden Sunset	Ex	Late May	Unusually large flowers of buff yellow with orange blotch.
Goldfinch	Kn	Late May	Apricot yellow flowers shading to pink. Tall grower.
Graciosa	Oc	Late May	Orange yellow flowers have a red suffusion and a tangerine orange blotch.
Hotspur Red	Ex	Late May	Very large trusses of orange red flowers touched with yellow on upper petals.
Irene Koster	Oc	May	Fragrant white flowers flushed soft pink.
Knap Hill Red	Kn	Early June	Small flowers of a brilliant deep red. Bronze leaves on a vigorous plant.
Koster's Brilliant Red	Mo	Early June	Blazing orange red 2½-inch flowers.
Lemonora	Mo	Late May	Flowers are apricot yellow shaded pink.
Magnifica	Oc	Late May	Rose red with orange yellow blotch.
Marina	Ex	Late May	Very large pale yellow flowers with pink shadings.
Marion Merriman	Kn	Early May	Rich yellow flowers with deeper yellow blotch.
Old Gold	Ex	Late May	Large golden yellow flowers.
Oxydol	Ex	April	Very large white flowers with yellow blotch in throat. Free-flowering plant with bronzy leaves.
Princess Royal	Ex	May	Huge fragrant ivory blooms faintly flushed pink open from pink buds.
Renne	Ex	May	Rich red flowers suffused with yellow. One of the earliest reds to bloom.
Rosella	Kn	Early June	Well formed large pale pink flowers; fragrant. Strong grower.
Royal Lodge	Ex	June	Very deep red flowers with long decorative stamens. Very late.
Strawberry Ice	Ex	May	Frilled trusses of coral pink flowers with yellow blotch on upper petals; 11 to 13 blooms to a truss.
Sun Chariot	Ex	May	Soft apricot yellow flowers on a compact, spreading plant.
Sylphides	Kn	Late May	Very light pink flowers with yellow shadings in the center.
Toucan	Kn	May–early June	Large fragrant creamy white flowers with big yellow blotch.
Whitethroat	Kn	Late May	Fragrant pure white double flowers. Compact plant has light green foliage. Flowers are smaller than most, but there are many of them.

Treasure chest of color
Woodland garden shelters thriving group
of azaleas and rhododendrons.
Deciduous yellow Mollis azalea is at right;
evergreen pink Rutherfordiana hybrid is at
center. Azalealike cloud of lavender in
background is *Rhododendron augustinii.*

THE VARIED EVERGREEN AZALEAS

Evergreen azalea hybrids stem from species native to eastern Asia. European and American hybridizers combined those species in various ways to produce strains that have specific growth and hardiness characteristics. Here are representatives of some of the most popular types (see page 12 for descriptions of the hybrid strains).

Formosa (Southern Indica)

Madonna (Brooks)

Mardi Gras

Gumpo Pink (Macrantha)

Mme. Alfred Sanders (Belgian Indica)

Tickled Pink (Rutherfordiana)

White Orchids (Gold Cup)

FLASHY DECIDUOUS AZALEAS

Brilliant shades of yellow and orange are the special contributions of deciduous azaleas, though they also come in white and soft pink tones. The various hybrid types are described on page 12.

Old Gold

Gibraltar

Mollis hybrid azalea

Exbury hybrid azalea

Rhododendron japonicum (foreground) and R. luteum

AZALEAS IN ACTION

Flowering azaleas become garden focal points, no matter what their color or how they're used. A single plant makes an arresting accent; and combined with other flowering plants, azaleas can be dominant features in tapestries of floral color.

Kurume azalea Ward's Ruby (foreground) and rhododendron Jingle Bells

Rutherfordiana azalea Alaska

Rhododendron augustinii (foreground) and Mollis hybrid azalea

Kurume azalea Hino-Crimson

Kurume azalea

Belgian Indica azalea

In nature's realm
Sunlight filtering through overhanging
trees, as in a native environment, lights up
brilliant rhododendron 'The Hon. Jean
Marie de Montague'.

Rhododendrons

To see most of the more than 900 rhododendron species in their native habitats, you would have to journey around the world. You might begin in Washington, Oregon or California; browse through Appalachia; go on to such exotic locales as Turkey and Armenia, Nepal, Sikkim, Tibet, even Afghanistan; and cover all of eastern Asia—from Siberia to New Guinea. The Himalayan frontiers of China and her southern neighbors are thought to be the homeland of the genus. Certainly this part of southeastern Asia features a greater number of species and natural hybrids per square mile than any other native habitat of rhododendrons: some of its intermountain valleys may contain as many as 200 species. But even with so many native floral treasures, eastern Asia was the last area to reveal her rhododendrons to Western plant explorers.

Rhododendrons in the Wild

An imaginary trip into the Himalaya mountains of northern India will give you a condensed view of the entire rhododendron clan; climbing upward through several types of forest and finally above the timberline, you'll encounter most of the variations in growth and flower styles that the genus has to offer. Because climatic conditions vary throughout the Himalayan range and the foothills on either side, no one part of the region can be designated as "typical." But a look at any place there will reveal the enormous diversity among rhododendron flower and plant types and growth patterns. Let's visit an imaginary location on the northeastern Burmese frontier.

At the lower elevations—which, depending on the region, may reach as high as 8,000 feet—rhododendrons are scattered among other kinds of plants and are quite inconspicuous when out of bloom.

The first species we encounter may be growing along—or even in—rocky stream beds. Climbing another one or two thousand feet, we're likely to smell the rhododendrons almost before we see them: whitish blossoms that resemble Easter lilies, on plants that clamber through tree and shrub branches. These are the tender, often epiphytic species that must be grown in greenhouses except in the mildest climates. And if we look up we may discover that we're walking *under* a rhododendron; the first tree-size species we encounter will appear in this constantly moist rain forest.

Climbing another thousand feet or so, we come into the heart of a temperate rain forest with a number of familiar trees: oaks, magnolias, and other broad-leafed evergreens with tree rhododendrons scattered among them. Numerous colorful flowering shrubs in the forest and on cliffsides catch the eye—more rhododendrons. At the upper limit of this forest, there are more species in colonies on rocky ridges; and dense, twiggy types begin to appear in thick tangles, by themselves or interlaced with dwarf bamboo.

Eventually, as we continue our upward climb, most broad-leafed trees give way to needle-leafed evergreens, predominantly firs. Among them are thickets and forests of rhododendrons: gnarled treelike specimens, scrubby types growing amid bamboo, and picturesque plants literally hanging from the cliffs and cascading over rocks. Early spring brings on a breathtaking spectacle of light green and bronzy new foliage, dark bluish green fir trees, and everywhere frothy billows of thousands of rhododendron flowers in scarlet, white, purple, pink, and lemon—all with flawless blue sky overhead.

Even above the timberline, rhododendron thickets 2 or 3 feet high persist, so dense that travel through them is difficult. Finally, in the last stronghold of high-altitude moorlands, where summers may be dry and snow covers the ground for 6 months a year, we'll find hundreds of square miles of alpine rhododendrons: plants no more than calf high clothing the rocks and meadows in all shades of pink through purple, with amber and gold for contrast.

By closely studying the Himalayan rhododendrons in the wild, plant explorer Frank Kingdon Ward determined that the more congenial a climate is for rhododendrons, the greater will be the number of species growing there—each species usually occupying only a small territory. Conversely, very few species will be found under borderline survival conditions, but they frequently extend over vast areas. Below the timberline in the Himalayas, adjacent hills or valleys may hold different species only in those locations.

Domesticating the Wild Rhododendrons

During their empire building in the 18th and 19th centuries, the English became the first to collect wild rhododendrons to introduce into gardens. The earliest exotic rhododendrons to reach Britain actually came from the Alps in 1656; then 80 years later four new species crossed the ocean—this time from the American colonies.

During the rest of the 1700s, an additional seven species came into cultivation—including, for the first time, some northern Asian varieties raised from seed sent to England by the German naturalist Pallas. Early in the 1800s, a few more new species reached English gardens—including those that would spark the explosion of rhododendron hybrids around 1830.

East meets west in early hybrids

The American *Rhododendron catawbiense*, which annually decorates the Appalachian mountains in clouds of pink, mauve, and lavender, arrived in England from North Carolina in 1809. Color purists today criticize the amount of blue in the pink flowers, but they don't deny that the Catawba rhododendron produces blooms in large, showy, compact trusses and—most importantly—on very hardy, adaptable, compact shrubs. The pioneer British hybridizer Michael Waterer anticipated the Catawba's value the year after its introduction and crossed it with the other large native of the eastern United States, *R. maximum*. This was the first careful attempt to guide rhododendron evolution.

The other species to ignite the imagination of rhododendron enthusiasts, sent to England in 1811, was *R. arboreum*. A tree in its native India, this was the first southeast Asian species to grow in English gardens. Fourteen years after its introduction, the first plants flowered—in dazzling scarlet.

Because the spectacular *R. arboreum* was too tender for all but the warmest coastal British gardens, several hybridizers tried to combine its blazing red color with a hardier plant; as other parents they used the Catawba rhododendron and several of its earlier hybrids. Their efforts resulted in hybrids with deep pink and red flowers; some of these are still grown today.

The real importance of the first English hybrids of Asian species, however, was that they suggested possibilities that might lie ahead. Even in the first-generation seedlings from the tender *R. arboreum*, hybridizers captured much of the color they sought on plants that could endure more severe winter cold. The excitement generated by these hybrids sent plant explorers into British India to ferret out more exotic species to put in the hybridizers' hands. The notable explorer Sir Joseph Hooker, for example, scouted the area of Sikkim and in 1850 sent to England 45 new species which he described and illustrated handsomely in *Rhododendrons of the Sikkim Himalaya*.

Throughout the rest of the 19th century, more new species were discovered and introduced (mostly from Asia), so that by 1900 some 300 were in cultivation. It was also during the latter part of the 19th century that extensive breeding programs produced a number of hybrids that even today are recommended (where they are hardy) as reliable, attractive garden rhododendrons—'Cynthia', 'Madame Mason', 'Mars', 'Pink Pearl', 'Purple Splendour', and 'Sappho', to name a few.

The 20th-century population explosion

With 300 species and numerous hybrids available at the turn of the century, it appeared that gardeners and hybridizers had at their disposal more than enough material to satisfy their horticultural and experimental desires. Few would have imagined that during the first two decades of the 1900s, plant-hunting expeditions would triple the number of available species.

The first plant explorer to assess the number of undiscovered species was Ernest H. Wilson. Hired by an English nursery to search for the fabled Dove Tree in China, he encountered an amazing variety of rhododendrons in the western Chinese provinces. Wilson sent back from his first expedition nearly as many new species as had Hooker 50 years earlier, and his three subsequent expeditions were as fruitful as the first.

Other courageous, dedicated, determined men in the employ of various nurseries, arboretums, and foundations made their mark through the quantity and quality of their discoveries in China, Burma, Tibet, and Bhutan. Even now it is exciting to imagine the thrill of being the first Westerner—knowing the value these new plants could have to horticulture—to glimpse, as did Frank Kingdon Ward, a miles-high moorland in western China covered with alpine rhododendrons in "a chromatic storm-tossed surf—rose, pink, purple, lavender, and amber, through which one may wade ankle deep for days on end."

Hybrids and hybridizers. The reputation of rhododendrons as a rich man's flower is not entirely unfounded, but not because rhododendrons are so difficult to grow or so initially expensive that only the wealthy can afford them. Rather, among private gardeners it was the wealthy and titled persons of the 19th and early 20th centuries who had the time to devote to growing and developing these plants, the land on which to do it (most of the earlier rhododendron hybrids and their parent species were large shrubs), and the money to hire the gardening staff needed to attend large collections of plants. Perhaps the most outstanding such person was the late Lionel de Rothschild, who assembled the world's largest (and possibly finest) rhododendron collection at his Exbury estate in England. With the best resources at his disposal and guided by impeccable taste, he produced numerous hybrids outstanding for their refinement and quality.

For nearly a century, however, professional nurserymen were responsible for most of the hybrids produced. In listings of standard hybrids, the names of Waterer and Slocock in England and Koster and van Nes in Holland appear again and again. Because the concern of these nurseries was commercial as well as aesthetic, they emphasized commercial advantages as much as beauty in their hybrids. They produced rhododendrons that were easy to propagate, with tough, adaptable, attractive plants; vigorous, trouble-free growth; and large flowers clustered in compact trusses.

Tomorrow's Rhododendrons

Because rhododendron hybridizers may experiment with such a vast number of species, the development of these plants might be considered as still at the threshold stage. And as gardeners discover the increasing number of colors and forms available and become familiar with basic cultural guidelines, the popularity of rhododendrons is bound to increase. Three particular trends in development promise to promote that popularity.

Emphasis on smaller plants. The discovery of the Asian rhododendrons during the first two decades of this century opened up many possibilities for colors, plant forms, and truss (or flower cluster) forms beyond the familiar English and Dutch nursery hybrids. The flood of new species included not only alpine dwarfs and forest giants but also numerous species of small to intermediate size—with smaller leaves than the typical nursery hybrids and with flowers in informal clusters. These have been taken in hand by a number of contemporary hybridizers concerned with developing smaller plants that will fit more comfortably into the ever-shrinking suburban garden.

Better plants from better parents. Continued explorations and the extensive culture of species from seed have demonstrated how variable most species of rhododendron are, and how important it is to use fine selected forms in hybridizing programs. The nursery trade now offers selections of many species—superior color variants, clones that flower more freely than usual, and plants with better growth habits. A classic example of the value of superior parent material is the superb assemblage of named hybrids in the 'Loderi' group. Their originator, Sir Edmund Loder, carefully chose the finest obtainable forms of *Rhododendrons griffithianum* and *fortunei* and produced from them, around 1901, a number of hybrids still unsurpassed for floral beauty and garden value.

Extension of growing range. With research, breeding, and dauntless experimentation by gardeners, the growing of rhododendrons has been extended into areas once thought unsuitable. Home gardeners, for example, have discovered by trial and error that many varieties will thrive under climatic conditions generally described as inhospitable. The growth in the popularity of rhododendrons in the southern United States—where soil fungi were thought to be a limiting factor—is proof that presumed obstacles can be overcome. Similarly, the heat of California's central valley and the alkaline water of the southern part of that state can now be handled in ways that allow gardeners in those areas to enjoy rhododendrons as permanent landscape features.

The dedicated efforts of amateur as well as professional hybridizers—developing new sorts that will perform faithfully in regions too cold, hot, or dry for a great number of available hybrids—have been indispensable. For every 'Scintillation' or 'Catalgla' that will survive $-25°F/-32°C$ winter temperatures, hundreds to thousands of seedlings must be planted and subjected to the trials of climate.

Rhododendrons in the Landscape

New rhododendron enthusiasts often think of these plants simply as compact, heavily foliaged shrubs that bear rounded trusses of large flowers— the typical English and Dutch nursery hybrids that grace many a public park. The differences between one rhododendron and another (save for color) may seem scarcely more than the differences between modern hybrid tea rose varieties.

With greater exposure to rhododendrons comes the thrilling revelation: the great variety in flowers, foliage, and growth that rhododendrons offer, from ground cover shrublets with needlelike leaves to large-leafed tree types, and the nearly complete range of colors.

Considering the variation in growth types alone, rhododendrons have nearly limitless landscape uses as long as growing conditions are favorable. There are rhododendrons that you can use as you would azaleas or floribunda roses—as low hedges to divide garden areas and as foreground border plants. The dwarf types are naturals for rock gardens. Those with lanky, pliable growth are effective when trained as espaliers on trellises or against protected walls. Larger sorts are admirably suited to serve as background shrubs in wide plantings and as screening shrubs. And the rhododendron setting *par excellence* is, of course, the woodland garden.

When shopping for rhododendrons, many gardeners are so dazzled by the blossoms that they fail to notice the variety of foliage colors and finishes, which can be nearly as important in the landscape (although more subtle) as any floral display. Just a little browsing will disclose a wide range of greens— light to very dark, with glossy to soft matte finishes—and some plants with leaves that are actually more blue or gray than green. With thoughtfully chosen background and companion plantings, such rhododendrons can be like jewels in an expensive setting, both in and out of bloom.

A number of rhododendrons have another feature that can be exploited by the clever gardener. On some species and their hybrids, the undersides of the leaves are covered with hair, like peach fuzz, called *indumentum*. Often orange, bronze, or silver in color, the indumentum contrasts handsomely with the green upper leaf surface. If these rhododendrons are planted where you can look up at the plant and see the undersides of the leaves, the effect can be striking. A number of rhododendrons produce new growth in orange, red, bronze, white, or chocolate hues that rival any floral display. With increased familiarity, you'll find rhododendrons so attractive in foliage and plant form that you'd cherish them even if they never bloomed.

Extending the season

Most nurseries that carry just a few rhododendrons offer the time-tested English and Dutch nursery hybrids, all of which come into glorious bloom at about the same time. The newcomer to rhododendrons may fail to realize that there are early and late-blooming species and varieties that will stretch the blooming season from January to September in mild climates, March to July where winters are more severe, even throughout the year with species and varieties in the Vireya section.

You can keep a particular garden vista in flower for several months simply by interplanting rhododendrons with different bloom seasons. By selecting plants carefully, you can even control the mood of your planting throughout the total bloom season: the earliest display might feature yellow, orange, cream, and salmon colors; this could be followed by reds, pinks, and blush whites; and the last burst might contain lavenders, purples, violets, and cream colors.

A word of caution. Consider the ultimate size of each rhododendron you select and the length of time it will take to attain that size. Too many windows have vanished behind foreground plantings, and too many potentially shapely specimen plants have been turned into grotesque parodies by overcrowding and competition for space. Although rhododendrons are easy to transplant, you can save yourself needless labor by choosing and planting wisely. Give your plants enough room to grow.

Rhododendron Care and Keeping

Although the 900 or so rhododendron species are found growing in many different natural situations—from alpine meadows to tropical rain forests, from near sea level to 18,000 feet—their basic requirements for healthy growth are the same everywhere.

Taking hints from the native environment

Any generalization about rhododendrons is bound to have at least one exception, but it's safe to say that most species are natives of mountains or foothills—which is the key to the five critical cultural requirements for the majority of the popular varieties:

1) well-aerated and highly organic soil (with a structure loose enough that air can enter pore spaces between particles as water drains out);
2) cool, moist soil (but well drained);
3) acid soil (pH 4.5–6.0);
4) shelter from wind and excessive sun;
5) cool, humid atmosphere.

Mountainous situations suggest land more sloping than level, with good drainage, and it is true that most rhododendrons are hillside shrubs. Also, at higher mountain elevations, temperatures are lower and rainfall higher, and under such conditions there is an accumulation of organic material; the abundant moisture promotes lush growth, but the organisms that break down dead leaves and branches that fall to the ground are less active at lower temperatures. The result is a loose soil composed largely of decaying organic material and always blanketed by a thick layer of dead leaves and twigs. The accumulation of organic matter gives the soil high acidity too: leaves and other plant remains release organic acids as they decompose.

Rhododendrons are shallow-rooted plants, their roots adapted to the porous but moist and highly organic soil of their native habitats. Dry soils and those that are poorly drained are fatal. And because their native soils are so loose, rhododendron roots are fibrous and fine-textured, unable to penetrate the dense soils found in many gardens.

The dependence of rhododendrons on abundant atmospheric moisture doesn't mean that you have to sprinkle their foliage every day it doesn't rain: many rhododendrons have minute hairs or scales on their leaf undersides that retard transpiration during dry spells. But a moist atmosphere is beneficial because it slows the rate of transpiration—that means that roots will draw water from the soil more slowly, and you won't have to water as frequently.

Wild rhododendrons do grow in full sun or in exposed locations, but in such cases they're the dominant—if not the only—plant in the area. Their numbers and density provide protection from the dehydrating action of sun and wind. Even so, the species that can survive in such situations are the exceptions. Most rhododendrons are forest plants,

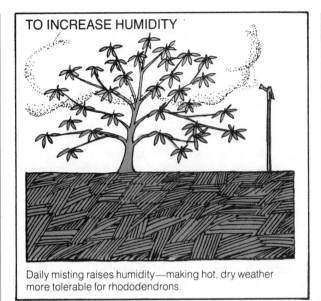

TO INCREASE HUMIDITY

Daily misting raises humidity—making hot, dry weather more tolerable for rhododendrons.

sometimes forming the dominant vegetation beneath broad-leafed or needle-leafed evergreen trees. As a general guide to the amount of exposure a rhododendron can tolerate, figure that the smaller-leafed sorts (which are usually the smaller-growing plants) can take more exposure: their small leaves present less surface area to the forces of dehydration.

Selecting a planting site

Rhododendrons are not difficult to grow as long as you cater to their few definite needs. The first requirements to consider are those that concern planting location.

Sunlight tolerance. The amount of sun a rhododendron can take without damage to the plant depends on the native habitat of a species or ancestry of a hybrid and on your local climate. Most rhododendrons should have as much sun as the foliage can withstand without burning or looking pale and unhealthy; sunlight promotes heavy flower production and compact growth, and helps plants mature properly and resist winter cold. A few species and hybrids are especially sensitive to sunlight and definitely require shade; this is noted in the descriptions on pages 44–48.

The amount of shade you'll need to give rhododendrons depends on the number of foggy, cloudy, or rainy days you can expect (on a yearly average) in your locality. The northern half of the United States' Pacific coast and much of Great Britain get more sunless days than does the United States' eastern seaboard. So a rhododendron planted in Baltimore will need more shade than one planted in Seattle. Many gardeners in the foggy Pacific coastal strip extending from Monterey north through

Oregon and Washington find that they can grow most rhododendrons in places that get full sun—when the sun shines. The more sunny days you can expect in a year, the more shade your rhododendrons will need. Where some protection from summer sun is needed, remember that afternoon sun is more intense.

Latitude is another factor to consider when you're deciding how much sun and shade to give your rhododendrons. As latitude increases on either side of the equator, the sun's rays strike the earth at greater and greater angles (from directly overhead); and the intensity of sunlight *decreases* as the angle of the rays increases. So rhododendrons in northern gardens actually need more sunshine each day than those in gardens further south.

Wind protection. Nearly all rhododendrons will appreciate being protected from the wind. Too much wind will increase a plant's transpiration rate to the point that roots cannot supply water as fast as leaves are losing it. This is an especially critical matter where soil freezes in winter: because shallow-rooted rhododendrons can't absorb moisture from frozen soil, winter wind can fatally dehydrate a plant.

You can use other kinds of plants to provide both an attractive background and protection to your rhododendrons. But be sure that the plants you group with your rhododendrons don't have shallow, invasive root systems.

A lath screen placed on the windward side of plants makes a good temporary shelter—until background plants develop—or even a permanent solution. Any protective screen or fence should be placed at a distance of about three times its height from the plants you want to shelter.

And as a general guide to wind tolerance, remember the rule of thumb mentioned on page 29: the types with smaller leaves need less shelter than those with large leaves.

Exposures. A northern exposure is often best for rhododendrons; sun rarely strikes the plant, but—if the site is open to the north—the amount of light received will be satisfactory for good growth. In cold winter regions, a north-facing slope is best because coldest air will drain away downslope, minimizing winter injury.

Eastern exposures are also generally successful, particularly where mornings are often overcast. In the eastern United States, however, early morning sun in the winter can damage frozen leaves and flower buds on early-flowering sorts by thawing them too rapidly. As long as cold-climate gardeners provide protection from the morning sun for early-blooming sorts, eastern exposures can be as satisfactory as northern.

A location facing west offers good sun and shade ratios; the problem with this kind of exposure is the afternoon heat when humidity is at its daily low point. Rhododendrons backed by shrubs or trees may succeed, but those placed against a west-facing wall will burn. Climate is a factor here, too; the greater the number of cool, overcast summer days, the more successful is a western exposure.

Southern exposures are almost always too hot unless you live in a fog belt or can provide high overhead shade.

Before selecting an exposure for your rhododendrons, be sure to check the direction of prevailing winds. A northern exposure buffeted by north winds will be of little advantage unless you provide plants with some sort of protection (see "Wind protection" at left).

Woodland plantings. Rhododendrons are, for the most part, woodland natives, so you can scarcely do better than plant them in the dappled sunlight of an open wood where treetops do not touch. The shelter of trees will make several degrees' difference in high summer temperatures and winter lows, and the changing patterns of sunlight falling on rhododendron leaves will eliminate the hazard of sunburn. Because a tree canopy also helps soil retain its warmth at night, a woodland location is especially good for hybrids or species that are subject to frost damage due to early spring growth or late ripening of growth in autumn.

The principal danger in woodland situations is too much shade. If necessary, thin out the trees before you set out your rhododendrons; removing trees from an established planting always involves some risk to the rhododendrons you want to help.

As a general rule, plant rhododendrons at least 5 or 6 feet from tree trunks. If you can place the plants where they'll have clear sky overhead, they'll benefit fully from rainfall and still get enough shade from nearby trees as light patterns change during the day.

Deep-rooted trees that cast filtered shade make the best woodland for rhododendrons. Mature oaks are excellent; as a bonus, their fallen leaves decompose slowly, providing a long-lasting mulch. Other good companion trees are dogwood (*Cornus*), silver bell (*Halesia*), snowbell (*Styrax*), and sour or black gum (*Nyssa sylvatica*). A number of needle-leafed evergreens, such as pines, Douglas fir, and coast redwood, offer good high shade, and their fallen needles make first-rate mulch; but they have dense networks of surface roots that extend some distance around each tree. With such trees, you have to locate rhododendron plants near enough to enjoy the shade but away from competitive root systems. Birches are attractive deciduous companion trees, but they, too, have shallow, competitive roots, and the same advice applies: place rhododendrons near enough to benefit from the shade but away from greedy roots.

Avoid such dense-foliaged or surface-rooted trees as ash, beech, elm, maple, poplar, pin oak, and sycamore. The leaves of the eastern black walnut and horse chestnuts release toxic substances during decomposition; and birches, lindens, tulip trees, and some oaks harbor insects that secrete a sticky, unsightly "honeydew" that can become a foothold for fungus diseases if not washed off foliage.

City dwellers can take advantage of manmade forests of buildings, which offer much the same protection from sun and wind as do woodland trees.

The best planting times

In the rhododendron country of the eastern United States—and in other regions with similarly chilly winters—many growers prefer to plant or transplant rhododendrons in early spring. This gives plants the most time to become established before the onset of freezing weather in autumn.

The Pacific Northwest (west of the Cascades) and most of California have winter weather that poses little hazard to most rhododendrons. But in many places within these mild-winter areas, the summers are hot, and in most of California there's no summer rainfall. In such locations, rhododendrons are better planted in late September or October so they can get established during the cool and moist winters. By the following summer, rhododendrons planted in autumn will be in better condition to withstand summer heat and dryness than will plants set out in spring.

Soil preparation

The description of rhododendrons' native environment (page 29) highlights the sort of soil these plants need: well-drained and well-aerated. Soil must be loose enough for the rhododendron's fine roots to penetrate easily, and it must be cool and moist (but not saturated) at all times. The key element in such soil is plenty of organic matter.

Organic materials, as they decompose, go through a cycle that differs only in length from one material to another. In the early stages, microorganisms remove nitrogen from the soil as they use it to do their work. Meanwhile, the decomposing materials release organic acids. This release of acids and the organisms' use of nitrogen both slow down as decomposition nears completion.

The nature of the decomposition process has two important implications for soil preparation. First, the organic matter you use to amend your soil for rhododendrons should already be partially decomposed, so that there will be less competition be-

tween plant roots and microorganisms for available nitrogen. Second, you should choose a material that's slow to break down; this will help keep the soil structure loose long enough for roots to get established in a well-aerated, well-drained environment. It will also maintain acidity while surface mulches (see page 35) begin breaking down and supplementing initial acidity.

One organic material that satisfies these requirements is good-quality peat moss. When you buy it, peat moss has already undergone considerable decomposition, but it will last for a number of years in the soil before completely breaking down. Various grades and types are sold; the more coarse-textured kinds will give you a looser, better-aerated soil structure than will the fine-textured ones. European sphagnum peat is usually the highest quality (and most expensive), and Canadian peats are also good choices. In the eastern United States and the Pacific Northwest, you may find locally produced peat that will be suitable.

Peat moss is not without a few drawbacks, though, especially when it makes up more than half the planting mix in raised beds or containers. To prepare peat moss for use, you have to squeeze water into it; if you just add water to dry peat, the peat will float. And therefore, soil amended with lots of peat must be kept moist; should it dry out, water will run off the surface. Moistening peat moss is easier if you add a small amount of a wetting agent to the water.

Many other materials give shorter-term benefits than peat moss but will work well as long as you follow a regular program of mulching and fertilizing. Partially decomposed pine needles are a good soil amendment, as are many by-products of regional agriculture, such as spent hops, soybean hulls, and grape or apple pomace; oak litter (leaves, twigs, and decaying smaller branches) is a fine soil amendment wherever available. Ground redwood, pine, or fir bark is increasingly popular.

Sawdust, as a soil amendment or as a mulch, is controversial. Gardeners on the west coast of North America—especially in the Pacific Northwest, where supplies are abundant—find that sawdust works well as a component of planting mixtures if it's well aged (partially decomposed) or if it's fortified with nitrogen to help it decompose. Without the addition of coarser organic materials, however, sawdust tends to create a soil that's too soggy for good root development; aged wood shavings or chips give a looser soil texture. Rhododendron growers in the eastern United States have had mixed results with plantings in soils conditioned with local pine sawdust. One problem is that growth is overstimulated by nitrogen fertilizers applied to counteract nitrogen depletion; freezing winter weather then damages plants with too much new growth.

Many eastern growers also report an unusual amount of rhododendron wilt on plants growing in soil amended with pine sawdust. Because of these risks, most easterners avoid using sawdust unless it's thoroughly aged.

Aeration and good drainage go hand in hand. To determine the sort of soil you have, dig a hole 18 inches deep and fill it with water; if within an hour the water is gone, your soil's drainage and aeration are satisfactory.

Soil that's too sandy is easier to adjust for rhododendron culture than is heavy clay. With sand you're assured of good drainage: the problem is ensuring moisture retention, which can be done by adding organic matter. Heavy clay soils, on the other hand, are more difficult to adjust because the soil surrounding your prepared area will always drain more slowly; small planting holes can become catch basins for water, drowning rhododendron roots in short order. Planting rhododendrons in raised beds or mounds of specially prepared soil will often be your best solution in heavy clay areas; this way, the rooting areas above the grade of surrounding soil will never be saturated for prolonged periods. For best results, raised beds should extend about 18 inches above the soil grade. Even so, you should also incorporate into the top 1 to 1½ feet of

RAISED BED PLANTING

Raised beds 18 inches above soil grade promote success with rhododendrons where heavy soil, alkaline water are problems.

native clay soil organic materials that will help improve its texture and permeability.

If you have only one or two plants to set out in heavy soil, you can generally achieve a satisfactory root environment if you dig a hole 18 inches deep and 2 feet wide. Check to be sure drainage is satisfactory; then fill the hole with a mixture of 40 percent organic material (at least half peat moss), 40 percent topsoil (not clay), and 20 percent sand. Be sure that this prepared soil rises significantly above the surrounding grade.

Because their root systems are not deep, rhododendrons can be grown over an alkaline soil with relative safety. Raised beds or mounds are the most satisfactory planting situation in alkaline areas and are good insurance against encroaching alkalinity from surrounding soil. Even with raised plantings, however, prepare the top 12 inches of native soil beneath the plantings with organic materials to improve soil texture.

Planting a rhododendron

A rhododendron from the nursery will almost always be either in a container or, if dug from a growing field, will have its root ball wrapped in burlap (known as "ball-and-burlap," or simply "b & b"). Regardless of its packaging, your first responsibility to a newly purchased rhododendron is to keep it moist until you can plant it.

As mentioned on page 29, the enemy of rhododendrons is poorly drained and poorly aerated soil. Improving the soil as suggested on pages 31–32 will help produce a soil structure to rhododendrons' liking; planting high, as shown in the illustration on page 33, will further ensure success. In sandy to loam soils, set each plant so that the top of its root ball is about one-third above the grade of surrounding unprepared soil. In time the prepared soil in which you plant the rhododendron may settle a bit, but the top of the root mass will remain somewhat above the surrounding grade. If you plant in heavy loam to clay soils, set the top of the root ball even higher—at least half its depth above the surrounding grade.

When the planting hole is ready to receive your rhododendron plant, remove the container or burlap from the root ball and carefully expose the root ends. If the plant is in loose, fibrous soil, you can gently break up the surface of the root ball with your fingers; an alternate method is to wash away some soil gently with water from a garden hose. Exposing their ends will encourage roots to reach out and establish themselves in their new location. If you have a plant that's been in its container so long that its roots are dense and matted, you can encourage them to extend into new soil with a careful root pruning. With a plant in a 1-gallon container, use a sharp knife to cut away ½ inch of matted roots from the edges of the root ball; cut away a 1-inch layer from plants in larger containers.

A newly planted rhododendron needs to be firmly anchored but not forced into the soil. After you place it in its planting hole, fill in around the root ball with prepared soil, lightly compacting the soil with your hands. Thoroughly water the soil to establish good contact between the root ball and surrounding soil. Never press in a plant by placing your foot on the root ball or on soil in the planting hole; the less the soil is compacted, the better will be aeration and drainage.

Transplanting a rhododendron

Their dense, fibrous root systems make rhododendrons among the easiest shrubs to transplant. Even large old specimens may be safely moved if the plant is in good health and you exercise reasonable care during the process.

You can dig up and relocate a rhododendron any time of the year when it's not in active growth and the ground isn't frozen. But you'll get the best results by transplanting according to the schedule proposed for setting out new plants in the garden (see page 31). Specimens in full bloom usually don't suffer much from a move, but plants moved while in bud may flower later than normal.

Generally, a rhododendron's root system extends outward as far as the spread of its branches, but when transplanting you can safely take a somewhat smaller root ball; a diameter equal to two-thirds the plant's height should be satisfactory. With a sharp spade, cut a circle with the desired diameter, to the spade's depth, around the plant. For small to medium-size plants (those with root balls up to about 2 feet across), the next step is to lift the plant carefully from the soil by inserting the spade underneath the root ball and using it as a lever to apply upward pressure—trying to keep the root ball intact.

If a plant is so large that the root ball might be broken by upward pressure, dig a trench to the spade's depth around the outside of the root ball and then undercut the root system so that the entire ball is cut loose from the soil. Carefully raise the root ball just enough to insert a partially rolled square of burlap halfway under the ball; then carefully raise the root ball from the opposite side and unroll the cloth the rest of the way so that the entire root ball is resting on the square of burlap. You'll need to use a piece of burlap large enough for you to lift the corners over the top of the root ball, tie opposite corners together, and then securely tie the whole wrapped root ball with twine so that it will hold together. Then the plant will be ready to be moved to its new location.

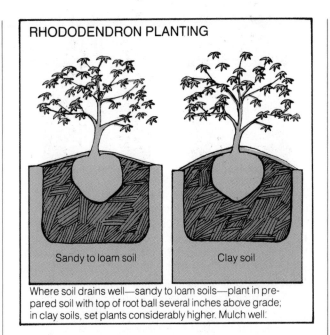

RHODODENDRON PLANTING

Sandy to loam soil | Clay soil

Where soil drains well—sandy to loam soils—plant in prepared soil with top of root ball several inches above grade; in clay soils, set plants considerably higher. Mulch well.

Even for medium-size plants which can be dug without the aid of burlap, it's good insurance to wrap the root ball once the plant is dug from the ground. Any jarring movement can break off part of the root ball; a burlap wrapping will help prevent this and will keep roots from being exposed should the root ball break up at all.

Be very careful if you lift a plant by its main stem when moving it from one place to another; a heavy root ball or a poorly attached root system can break. You can move large, heavy plants across a garden on a pallet made from a sheet of plywood or lightweight metal or even on a heavy tarpaulin.

Replanting a rhododendron transplant is just like planting a new one from the nursery, as described on page 32. If you've wrapped the root ball in burlap, remove as much of it as you can without disturbing the root system so that the sides of the root ball will be exposed to the soil you'll fill in around it.

Watering

If you'll keep in mind that rhododendrons need soil that's well-drained and aerated but never absolutely dry, you'll understand their water needs: enough water, applied often enough, that the soil is never either dry or saturated for any length of time. How often you should water will depend on how quickly the soil approaches dryness, and that in turn will depend on a number of factors: plant location (how much sun or shade), climate (humidity, amount of overcast), and presence or absence of a mulch (see page 35). The surest test for moisture content is simply to feel the soil. But if you neglect to water them for too long, the plants will let you know: leaves that

Growing rhododendrons is easiest in those parts of the country where rhododendrons grow wild. Even though such areas won't be congenial to all the Asian rhododendrons and their hybrids, you can be sure that they have a basic "rightness" of soil, atmosphere, and moisture that will satisfy at least some rhododendrons with a minimum of help from you.

The basic factor limiting your choice of varieties will be winter cold: the temperate environment of, say, San Francisco will allow you a much wider choice than will the more bracing climate of Boston or Cleveland or even Seattle.

It's not that you can't grow rhododendrons well in other areas. But the farther you are from rhododendrons' "natural" homes, the closer attention you must pay to the plants' basic needs (see pages 29–31) and the more care you must take to compensate for the needs your region doesn't satisfy—for example, humidity, coolness, and acid soil. Gardeners have been successfully growing rhododendrons for years in such seemingly improbable places as Kansas, Oklahoma, Illinois, and Minnesota.

If you wish to experiment with growing rhododendrons in a less than ideal climate, begin with the "ironclad" hybrids of *Rhododendron catawbiense*. The old Catawba hybrids are not just generally the most cold-tolerant; they're also quite rugged overall—able to withstand heat, dry atmosphere, and poorer soil better than most others.

Further recommendations of good performers for various regions of the United States appear in *American Rhododendron Hybrids,* published in 1980 by the American Rhododendron Society (see address on page 2).

droop below their normal position are a sign that the plant needs water right away.

Mulches

A constant mulch is essential to successful rhododendron culture. In the wild (see page 29), rhododendrons grow with a blanket of leaves over their roots; while the lower layer decomposes, a new supply is falling to replace those that eventually become part of the soil. As the leaves (or needles) in a mulch break down, they create a loose, fibrous layer for roots to grow into, and release organic acids that help give soil the acidity necessary for proper nutrition. A good, thick layer of mulch keeps soil cool during the day and warmer than unmulched soil during the night; it also conserves moisture.

Oak leaves (particularly those from evergreen oaks), pine needles, and wood chips, twigs, and branches are top choices for mulching rhododendrons, although the leaves of most hardwood trees and needle-leafed evergreens make satisfactory mulching material. (A notable exception is maple leaves: they compact to form an airtight mat and break down too quickly to be of any lasting value.) Coarse ground bark and bark chips (available in several sizes) may be sold at nurseries and garden centers. Each is attractive, long-lasting, and no barrier to water penetration.

Regional agriculture will offer additional mulching materials. Ground sugar cane stalks, ground corncobs, and grape pomace are just three examples.

Peat moss is difficult to use as a mulch. If it dries out, it forms a surface layer that's nearly impervious to water; and because it breaks down so slowly, it's of little value in providing organic acids.

In general, avoid any fine-textured materials, like sawdust, that will pack down to form a smothering layer that water and air cannot penetrate.

Application and timing. The ideal mulching materials—pine needles or wood chips, for example—that permit free penetration of water and air can be spread over the soil in a layer 3 to 4 inches thick.

You can apply a mulch at any time of the year. Since deciduous trees drop their leaves in autumn, this would seem to be a "natural" time to apply mulches and is preferred in regions that have winter snowfall. In such areas, a mulch renewed in autumn, which will add protection in winter (see page 41), can be applied thickly enough to reach the lowest leaves on the plants. By springtime, such a thick mulch may have been reduced to about half its autumn depth, and any in excess of about 2 inches can be removed after the danger of freezing has passed.

Rhododendron growers in warmer climates—especially where summers are dry and hot—should mulch plants before the onset of warm weather.

Mulches help control weeds; they prevent seeds from germinating and form a loose rooting medium that makes any weeds that do appear very easy to pull. A mulch will also check the overzealous gardener who might be tempted to cultivate the soil under rhododendrons. Such cultivation will injure the surface network of roots, hindering rather than helping a rhododendron's growth. Any weeds that appear should be pulled by hand.

Periodically check your mulch to be sure it covers the soil surface completely. Squirrels and large birds can scratch away enough mulch to expose surface roots to drying air.

Nutrients and fertilizers

Many gardeners think of fertilizers as a cure for all problems—the first and last resort for making a sick plant well and a healthy plant healthier. But plants, unlike animals, manufacture some of their own nutrients and don't need to be continually supplied.

Why fertilize? Because soils don't always dependably supply enough of the essential nutrients plants need, fertilizers may be necessary as supplements for better growth. An intelligent fertilizer program is based on knowledge of what nutrients are needed for overall plant health, the times of year when plants may need them, and when *not* to fertilize.

Rhododendrons are not heavy feeders. If your plants are flowering well and producing satisfactory amounts of healthy new growth each year (6 to 8 inches for the larger-leafed kinds, less for smaller ones), you probably don't need to help them along. At most they'll need a light application of a complete acid fertilizer (see page 36).

Nutrients and timing. The three major plant nutrients are nitrogen, phosphorus, and potassium (usually referred to as potash). Nitrogen speeds vegetative growth and gives leaves a rich green color. Phosphorus promotes root activity and the ripening and maturing of plant tissues, and is necessary for flower and fruit production. Potassium encourages the development of plant tissues and the manufacture of sugars and starches within the plant.

Plants need nitrogen most when they're beginning active growth and throughout the growth period. Outdoors, a growth period is triggered by the proper combination of temperature, moisture, and day length: for most plants this occurs in spring, when the weather is warming and moisture is plentiful.

At other times of the year, when the weather is as warm or warmer than early spring and if moisture is available, an application of nitrogen will trigger more new growth. In a greenhouse or a frost-free climate, this can be an advantage: you can push plants to grow to larger size in less time. But for most rhododendron growers, new growth late in the season is a potential problem rather than a blessing. Summer temperatures increase transpiration rates, and young growth will wilt easily unless watering is carefully tended. Late growth has less time than does spring growth to mature properly before the onset of cool autumn weather; and where frosts or freezing winters are common, unripened growth is likely to be damaged or killed.

Because rhododendrons initiate new growth right after bloom, this is the time of year they use nitrogen most and may need a supplement to that available naturally. You have a choice of several approaches to nutrient application.

Complete fertilizers specially formulated for acid-loving plants (camellias, rhododendrons, and azaleas) provide the three major nutrients in a balanced formula suitable for these plants. Avoid using ordinary complete fertilizers (''rose food'' or ''vegetable food,'' for example) because they may contain nitrogen in a form that will leave an alkaline rather than acid residue. You can apply a complete fertilizer just as flower buds swell, and repeat applications monthly until new growth gets underway in the later spring.

Another way to provide nutrients is to supply the three major ones separately—or at least not all combined in one complete formula. For example, you might first apply only ammonium phosphate, for nitrogen, and follow at monthly intervals with a complete acid fertilizer that's lower in nitrogen and contains phosphorus and potassium. Ammonium phosphate is a good inorganic nitrogen source because it releases its nitrogen quickly and leaves an acid residue.

A grower in coastal central California has worked out a fertilizing schedule that suits a climate where severe frosts are not a problem. Right after bloom he applies ammonium phosphate, with another application three weeks later to plants that don't respond to the first. A month after the first ammonium phosphate application comes the first in a series of monthly applications of a commercial formula containing phosphorus and potassium in equal amounts. The time for the last such application in his area is late November. With both fertilizers—ammonium phosphate and the phosphorus-potassium combination—the gardener allows plants a tablespoon for each foot of height, scattered beneath the plants and watered in thoroughly.

Organic nitrogen sources, including cottonseed meal, fish meal, tankage, and fertilizers containing urea formaldehyde (U.F.), release nitrogen more slowly than do the inorganic fertilizers; the stimulus is weaker but lasts longer.

Use any fertilizer only in the quantity recommended on the packages—or even less. Small and young plants in particular are often sensitive to excessive amounts of fertilizers. When in doubt, use a light hand. Apply all fertilizers directly on top of mulch and water in thoroughly.

Where winters are cold. In areas with severe winters, apply nitrogen only up to mid-June; growth stimulated after the normal first flush is liable to injury by winter weather. You can continue to apply phosphorus and potassium later—until the end of summer—to help mature the season's growth. Those two nutrients are generally available combined in equal proportions in a formula without nitrogen, such as 0-10-10.

Liquid fertilizers. Plants absorb liquid fertilizers immediately and begin to show results quickly; the granulated sorts you apply to the soil may not take effect for a week or more and may make nutrients available to plants longer than you wish. With liquid fertilizers you also have much tighter control over the quantity of fertilizer you give your plants; if you follow recommendations for diluting, you'll avoid most risk of burning your plants.

Spraying or drenching leaves with liquid fertilizer can be beneficial in certain cases. Some broad-leafed rhododendrons and the epiphytic species and their hybrids normally receive some nutrients through their foliage, although nature doesn't provide the carefully balanced formulations and optimum strengths that commercial liquid fertilizers do. You can measurably increase the growth of young plants by following a regular program of spraying liquid fertilizer on the foliage, in concentrations somewhat lower than those recommended for soil application. Until midsummer you can make applications as frequently as every two weeks. Rhododendrons with waxy, slick leaves will benefit the least from nutrients applied to the foliage.

The best times for spraying on liquid fertilizers are evenings, early mornings, or other periods of high humidity and little or no strong or direct sunlight on the foliage. On sunny days, leaves rally all their defenses against excessive transpiration; but in the cool dampness of mornings, evenings, and cloudy days, they're much more receptive to moisture. The most efficient spray coverage is possible when the air is still, and mornings and evenings usually are the times of day with the least air movement. In very moist or humid regions, gardeners often prefer to spray in early morning rather than late in the day. In such climates, wet foliage at night may encourage fungus diseases.

A commercial spreader-sticker or a teaspoon of household detergent added to each gallon of fertilizer solution will help the solution spread more evenly over the leaves. Some growers in humid climates forego this, however, feeling that spreader-sticker agents provide a foothold for fungus diseases.

Pruning rhododendrons

If you have watched over your rhododendrons since their infancy—guiding their progress by judicious pinching—your pruning chores will be limited to emergencies. Of course, if you have inherited a garden with rangy old plants or shrubs that were planted with no respect for their ultimate sizes, you'll need to know how to bring these rough gems back to their deserved polish as garden ornaments.

Pinching: Preventive maintenance. Some rhododendrons are naturally leggy in growth habit, and others branch readily and grow into compact, bushy plants. When you understand how rhododendrons grow, however, you can shape potentially leggy plants into a well-balanced specimens by pinching or breaking off leaf buds in the first two or three years of growth.

A typical leggy plant looks like the one shown on page 38 after four cycles of growth. Occasional branching will occur, but in many cases stems will continue to form with no branches.

The terminal buds (which were at points A) were leaf buds; in the spring these extend upward in a slim sharp point. If undisturbed they break into leaf and grow a stem that is from several inches to a foot long, depending on the species or hybrid and culture. As this growth cycle is completed in May or June, the leaves will attain full size, and growth will stop while the wood hardens. The new shoots will

REMOVING OLD BLOSSOMS

To remove spent bloom truss (a process called "dead-heading") after flowering, break if off just below lowest flower and above small new growth buds.

form terminal buds (at points B), which may be either leaf or flower buds.

If the buds at B are leaf buds and are left alone, the plant will produce another cycle of growth (3) without branching. If the plant is growing vigorously, two cycles (or more, in mild climates) of growth (2 and 3) may occur in one year—one cycle completed in May or June and the next in July or August. The fourth growth cycle, in the following spring, may continue without branching as in 4, or produce branches as in 4a.

In order to encourage branches to form, pinch terminal buds—unless they are round, fat, blunt-tipped flower buds—as growth begins to elongate in spring. This will force several shoots to develop from dormant eyes in the lower leaf *axils* (where leaves join the stem). Leaf buds produce a plant hormone that inhibits development of dormant buds along the stem; flower buds don't produce this hormone, which is why a number of shoots usually grow from lower leaf axils on branches that have flowered.

If you're training a young plant (12 to 18 inches at time of purchase), continue this pinching procedure after each growth cycle for 2 or 3 years. By then you'll have a filled-out shrub that will produce many more flower buds than a plant of similar age that's been left to its own devices.

After such initial training, your rhododendron's basic structure will be established. Occasionally, you may need to pinch leaf buds that would grow to unbalance the plant; however, since healthy rhododendrons produce more terminal flower buds and fewer terminal leaf buds as the plants grow older, the need for attention to training will steadily decrease.

Pruning: Restorative maintenance. The gardener who has inherited a planting of rhododendrons frequently faces problems that require solutions more drastic than the procedures outlined above. For want of early training, the shrubs may have reached a gangly middle age, marring the landscape or hiding windows they were never meant to cover. Or the previous gardener, full of good intentions, may have overwatered, overfertilized, or planted his rhododendrons in more shade than they required; singly or in combination, such mistakes can produce rangy, unbranched plants. To restore plants to their rightful attractiveness, you'll need pruning shears and courage.

Growth buds on rhododendron plants form in the leaf axils. Leaves are produced in clusters or rosettes at the ends of branches and usually persist for several years. Consequently, a 3-year-old unbranched stem may have three or more rosettes of leaves: one at the branch terminal and the others lower on the branch, with bare stem between. Small

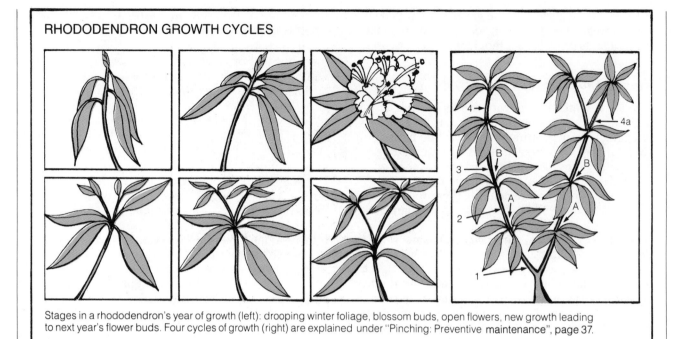

RHODODENDRON GROWTH CYCLES

Stages in a rhododendron's year of growth (left): drooping winter foliage, blossom buds, open flowers, new growth leading to next year's flower buds. Four cycles of growth (right) are explained under "Pinching: Preventive maintenance", page 37.

scars along bare sections of stem are not dormant growth eyes; they're left over from bud scales that enclosed the leaf bud before it elongated.

If you need to perform only minor repairs in order to shape up your rhododendron, make your cuts just above the leaf rosettes, and new growth will emerge from the dormant eyes there.

Major surgery, on the other hand, requires more time and observation. When you have to cut into a branch below any leaf rosettes, look for faint rings on the bark where there once were leaves— they mark the ends of previous growth periods. Careful inspection should reveal small bumps, which are growth buds under the bark. Make your cuts just above the rings so that dormant buds below them will be stimulated into growth.

If you can't find any rings or dormant buds on bare branches, make your cuts wherever you must in order to shape your rhododendron; later, when new growth starts, remove all branch stubs above the new growth. As a general rule, however, don't leave branch stubs above leaves or dormant eyes; they only die back to the point where new growth emerges.

Should you plan to renew a rhododendron by heavy pruning, you'll get best results by removing one-third of the plant each year over a 3-year period. The entire plant may be cut back in one operation— and sometimes you may have to treat a damaged plant this way—but you'll lose all flowers for a year or two and run a greater risk of killing the plant. Be sure to cut out old weak stems entirely. These will

not improve with better care and are best replaced by new growth that will respond to good culture.

Dormant buds should begin to grow within a month on smaller limbs or 10 weeks on tall main trunks. Occasionally, an old plant given major surgery will fail to put out any new growth; in these cases, reduce unpruned branches to the height of those pruned.

Some growers have found that an application of a fertilizer containing only nitrogen and phosphorus (such as 16-20-0) at the time of pruning will stimulate new growth on a heavily pruned rhododendron that is reluctant to send out shoots from old, bare wood. If the plant still refuses to grow, this usually indicates it has been severely weakened by insects, disease, or malnutrition. In such cases you're generally better off starting over with a young, vigorous plant, giving it careful training during its formative years.

Certain species and named rhododendron hybrids respond poorly or not at all to pruning. Members of the Falconeri series (and tree rhododendrons in general) will not produce new growth from bare wood; rhododendrons in the Thomsonii series also resent pruning. Smooth-barked rhododendrons put out little, if any, growth from stumps. All such species and hybrids will have to be trained from youth if they are to become well-balanced, compact plants.

When to prune. Winter or early spring is the preferred pruning season in mild climates; spring, after frost no longer threatens, is best where winters are severe. Because dormant growth buds start to mature following pruning, winter or early spring pruning will stimulate them to grow when the season begins. This is especially important in areas having inhospitable winters, as it gives new growth the longest time possible to grow and mature before the onset of cold weather. Avoid autumn pruning in cold-winter climates: cold damage is more severe around pruning wounds than on unpruned parts of the plants.

Cutting rhododendron trusses for spring bouquets is an excellent way to do some minor pruning to shape up a plant. Irregular growths of the last year or two, which destroy the symmetry of a plant, are especially good candidates for cut flowers. Remember to make all cuts just above a rosette of leaves.

Troubleshooting Rhododendron Health Problems

Most of our favorite ornamental plants play host to a few particular insects and disease organisms. Rhododendrons are no exception; but only a few of the pests and diseases presented in the chart on page 10 are considered potentially serious, and of those, some appear only in specific regions of the country.

More often than not, poor health in a rhododendron stems from poor culture or some sort of environmental trouble. Problems stemming from above-the-ground environmental conditions are presented in the paragraphs that follow. For discussion of problems that are soil related, refer to pages 10–11 in the Azaleas chapter.

Chlorosis

Symptoms of chlorosis are pale leaves with leaf veins standing out in contrasting darker green (see illustration on page 40). Causes and treatments are outlined on pages 10–11.

Sunburn

Damage from the sun appears as brown patches on leaves—round spots along edges and tips from the summer sun, and elongated patches on either side of the mid-vein when winter sun is intense and soil is frozen. Rarely of major importance in themselves, damaged spots offer a foothold for the establishment of secondary fungus infections which can weaken the plant.

Any sunburn is the result of transpiration that proceeds faster than roots can resupply leaves with water. Your first line of defense is to see that plants have adequate moisture for their locations. Especially if your soil is likely to freeze during the winter, be sure your plants are well watered just before freezing weather arrives.

Although rhododendrons require plenty of light for best performance, too much sun works against them; remember that the larger the leaves, the less direct sun the plant needs. If you determine that your plants are receiving too much sun, you would be wise to provide additional shelter or move them to a shadier location.

Three other variables influence a plant's sun tolerance. Gardens near water (or within a few miles of large bodies of water) generally have enough moisture in the air that a given rhododendron can take more direct sun than it could in a drier atmosphere. The age of a plant and how long it has been established in its location influence its sensitivity to all conditions; young and newly planted specimens are more subject to damage than are older, established plants. Finally, some varieties are inherently susceptible to sun burn.

Windburn and salts injury

These two problems, arising from different causes and requiring different treatments, both produce damage similar in appearance. To determine which is affecting your plants, look at which growth is injured: browned margins and tips on older leaves indicate salts damage; new growth with browned edges has windburn.

The remedy for windburn is fairly simple: give your plants some protection until you have a chance to move them to a more congenial location. The causes and remedies of salinity are discussed on page 11.

Frost damage and winter injury

This is one of the recurring problems that gardeners in cold-winter climates learn to live with. Winters themselves you can anticipate, and provide suitable protection for tender plants; it's the unusually early autumn frosts and unexpected late spring ones that do the damage.

Frost injury assumes several forms, depending on its severity. Leaves may look distorted and rough, or they may be killed outright; sometimes spring frosts will kill new growth on leaf tips and edges while leaf bases and new stems remain undamaged, because new leaves fold over one another like scales, protecting the bases of those higher on the stem.

If a particular plant is consistently injured by frost each year, it's too tender for the site where it's growing and possibly for your part of the country. Move it to a more sheltered place in your garden, avoiding low spots with no air circulation which become frost pockets in cold weather.

Injury from low winter temperatures is easily recognizable: flower buds are killed and turn brown, or blisters appear along leaf margins. Such damage has little effect on the overall health of your rhododendrons; it's the less obvious kinds of injury that can be fatal.

Freezing temperatures are especially dangerous to unprotected branches and main stems, causing the bark to split and separate from the body of the stem. In severe cases the bark will pull away all the way around the limb and everything above that point will die; in cases of moderate damage, the bark splits and rolls back but not all the way around the branch. Such injuries are deceptive: affected branches may not die until the following summer, going unnoticed in the meantime while hidden by foliage.

Sometimes freezing conditions will only split the bark without causing it to separate from the core. These wounds often callous over and allow the plant to function normally, but until the cracks heal they provide easy entry for fungus infections. Grafting wax or even paraffin painted onto the cracks will help the healing process and prevent diseases from entering.

Although some rhododendrons damaged by winter cold may sprout anew from their bases if you cut them down, there is usually no effective remedy for injury caused by freezing. All you can do is try to prevent winter damage by coordinating the growth of your rhododendrons with the growing season in your area (see pages 41–42) and to provide winter protection, where necessary, for your plants (page 42).

Failure to bloom

Often young rhododendron plants spend their first several years in the garden establishing a framework of limbs at the expense of flower buds. This tendency will vary somewhat according to variety; some species raised from seed may require 5 to 15 or more years to reach blooming age.

Shade is probably the most frequent cause of low bloom production on established plants. Sunlight, or at least *light*, is required to set flower buds for the following spring; too much sun burns foliage, too little cuts down on flowers. This is largely a matter of trial and error, the solution depending on your location and varieties. For more information on sun-to-shade ratios, see "Selecting a planting site" on page 29.

Although rhododendrons require nitrogen for healthy growth and bloom (see pages 35–36), over-fertilization with high-nitrogen fertilizers will produce vegetative growth in place of flower buds. Unless you live in a mild-winter climate, these plants will also be more subject to winter damage. The remedy is to reevaluate your fertilizing program: cut down on nitrogen or eliminate it temporarily, but maintain applications of phosphorus and potassium, which will promote flower formation and ripening of growth.

Rhododendrons are prodigious seed-setters, and producing large quantities of seed takes a lot of energy that the plant would otherwise use to form flower buds for the next year. An annual spring garden job, then, is to remove faded rhododendron bloom trusses (called "deadheading," see illustration page 37), especially on young plants. Failure to do so may lead to heavy flowering every other year with few blooms in between.

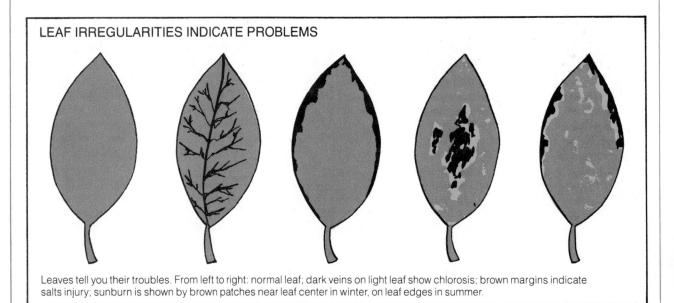

LEAF IRREGULARITIES INDICATE PROBLEMS

Leaves tell you their troubles. From left to right: normal leaf; dark veins on light leaf show chlorosis; brown margins indicate salts injury; sunburn is shown by brown patches near leaf center in winter, on leaf edges in summer.

You can minimize your autumn garden chores if you understand the factors that affect a plant's hardiness. Some varieties may always be tender unless they are somehow protected, but those of marginal hardiness can be placed and cared for in a way that will promote adaptation to your climate and thereby reduce the care they require over the winter. Even notably hardy specimens will benefit from your gardening savvy in exceptionally cold years.

In essence, you want to give your rhododendrons a winter environment where temperature fluctuations will be both more gradual and less extreme than in an exposed area.

In a "normal" season, more plants are probably lost to rapid temperature changes than to low temperature alone. Water is expelled from plant cells into intercellular spaces as temperatures fall; this water then freezes. And when a plant is suddenly exposed to a rise in temperature, it begins transpiring, but the cells aren't able to regain water fast enough. The result is a wilted leaf, followed in time by a desiccated plant.

Preventive measures

How do you provide protection from rapid temperature changes? You might cover or shelter all your rhododendrons, but since this involves the greatest amount of work, let's examine some preventive measures first.

Before you plant a rhododendron, carefully analyze the exposure of the planting site. Your problems will be greater if you select a site that encourages late autumn and early spring growth. Planted against walls facing south, for example, rhododendrons will be tempted to grow during more of the year than plants facing north. In northern exposures, greater shade or less direct light slows growth earlier in autumn and shields plants from premature springtime warmth. Similarly, plants growing under a canopy of trees or in partial shade of other plants will enter dormancy earlier than specimens in the open garden and will respond later to spring warmth.

Where early morning sun strikes frozen leaves and flower buds, damage will be more severe than in locations where the air temperature rises gradually. For this reason unsheltered eastern and southern exposures are less desirable for early-flowering sorts than northern or western exposures in the eastern United States and other cold-winter areas where sunny winter mornings outnumber cloudy ones.

Any warm, sunny spot or location open to frequent winds will accelerate water loss from plant tissues; if soil freezes through the root zone, there is no way for plants to resupply the lost moisture. Wind protection can be supplied by topography, buildings or fences, or other plantings.

Mulches moderate temperature extremes in two ways. They maintain a more constant soil temperature than in unmulched areas, and they can prevent the ground from freezing to any great depth. A mulched plant with its lower roots extending into unfrozen soil can supply moisture to transpiring leaves.

Finally, never plant rhododendrons in the lowest part of the garden—especially if it's a flat or "hollow" area with little or no air circulation. Since cold air—like water—seeks the lowest possible level, plants in your lowest garden spots will be the most likely to freeze.

Summer care ... where soil freezes in winter

One cardinal rule of rhododendron culture is to keep the root zone moist (not wet) and cool. It may come as a surprise, then, to be told to taper off on water in August, but this is a technique that some growers in areas of frozen winter soils use to prepare plants for winter cold. If combined with a fertilizing schedule that won't promote late-season growth, it will slow the plant's growth and promote a buildup of sugars in their cells. These cells will then withstand freezing temperatures better than those rich in water and low in sugars.

Tapering off on watering sets in motion a "water-deficit" process. As a plant draws water from the soil, the upper half of the root zone dries out first because more roots are active there. When the upper roots exhaust the moisture available to them, the plant becomes dependent on the fewer lower roots. With fewer roots supplying water, the plant approaches a point where the water supply wavers between adequate and inadequate. The leaves remain turgid on cool days but wilt on hot days. Or there may be just enough water to keep the leaves from wilting except in the hottest part of a warm August day. This water deficit slows the growth process; a plant near the wilting point functions fewer hours per day than does a plant with a water supply adequate for any emergency.

New leaves that droop during the day but return to their normal freshness in the evening tell you the plant still has enough moisture in reserve; should they remain limp, you know it's time to add more water. Where summers are cool or moist (but winters are freezing), rhododendron growers often give their plants an early evening foliage spray to perk up drooping leaves. Gardeners in hot-summer climates where leaf burn is a summer problem may employ a morning or evening foliage spray routinely so that leaves will not wilt during the day:

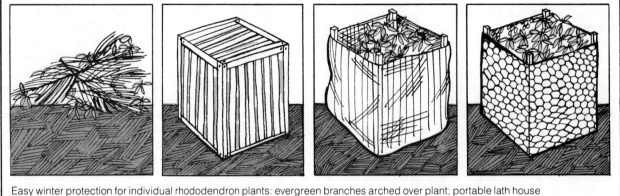

FOUR FORMS OF WINTER PROTECTION

Easy winter protection for individual rhododendron plants: evergreen branches arched over plant; portable lath house made from crate; burlap surrounding (but not touching) shrub; cage of poultry netting to hold insulating oak leaves.

wilted leaves burn more readily than those with enough moisture to remain turgid.

Whenever foliage sprays become inadequate to prevent new leaves from wilting, plants will need to be watered thoroughly so that moisture will be sure to reach the lowest roots. Following this, the foliage spray routine should be resumed.

Early August is the usual time to begin tapering off on water. By the time you can expect the first autumn frosts, nights will have cooled enough that the danger of growth stimulation is past; you can then resume normal watering. Take special care that your rhododendrons are well-watered before soil freezes for the winter. During that period the plants will have to depend on whatever moisture is in their tissues—roots can't extract any more water from frozen soil.

Two other steps in good rhododendron culture, if observed, will contribute to the success of a water-deficit program. A good, well-drained soil prepared to a depth of about 2 feet will promote the development of lower roots on which a thirsty plant can depend when surface roots can no longer supply water. A mulch over the planting area will maintain a cool root zone and minimize water loss from evaporation.

Caution: new plants. Newly planted specimens should be spared the water-deficit treatment. You may have to water them regularly during their first season, as their root systems won't be established enough to withstand an enforced drought. These plants will usually be small enough that you can easily shelter them during their first winters.

Protective devices

The theory behind the physical protection of plants during winter is the same as that discussed under "Selecting a planting site" (see page 29). Crates, frames, and screens all serve to slow down temperature fluctuations. If you've exercised care in locating your rhododendrons, such measures may be necessary only for the first few years—with tender sorts—until the plants are definitely established. If, however, you've inherited plants that are unwisely placed for winter survival and it's too late to move them, protective devices may save your plants until spring, when you can relocate them.

In areas with cold winters or hot, unfriendly summers (regardless of winter temperatures), lath houses may provide enough protection for gardeners to grow varieties otherwise sensitive to such climates. Rhododendrons that are too tender for exposed sites are often grown successfully in lath houses. These can provide ample shelter during cold winters—even when the plants are planted in the ground. Certainly in areas with hot or dry summers, the protection from sun and wind provided by a lath house reduces transpiration rates significantly, to the great benefit of the plants. Experimenters in the Midwest and central California have found lath houses to be especially helpful. The improved summer growth under lath probably better prepares the plants for withstanding winter severities.

Portable Color from Container Plants

Although many gardeners would think of azaleas rather than rhododendrons as prime container subjects, there's no reason why, with careful selection, rhododendrons couldn't be as popular and as widely used. Of course, the massive shrub and tree types are less suited to container culture (unless you have a large container and plenty of space); but as pointed out on pages 25–26, the genus Rhododendron contains many species and countless hybrids that range from medium-size to ground cover sorts, with various growth habits as well. Species in the Edgeworthii, Maddenii, and Cinnabarinum series—and hybrids of these—often make leggy or vinelike plants that can be grown in tubs and trained as informal espaliers against cool house or patio walls. Some of the small ground cover sorts will cascade over the edges of a pot or tub. Members of the Vireya section (those popularly called "Malesians") are not only excellent container subjects but can also be grown as indoor plants. And of course the small to medium-size shrubby sorts can offer abundant color in season and beautiful foliage for the rest of the year.

Culture and landscape uses for container-grown rhododendrons are the same as for azaleas grown in containers. For a full explanation and directions, refer to page 7.

RHODODENDRON SHOPPING GUIDE

Shopping for rhododendrons can be, literally, a beautiful experience. But it can also be somewhat bewildering if you're confronted with an assortment of varieties about which you know nothing. The listings on the following pages include the most popular and widely grown varieties, giving descriptions of plants and flowers, sizes, bloom seasons, and hardiness. The following paragraphs clarify the abbreviated information given in the listings.

Rhododendron quality ratings. Some years ago the British Rhododendron Society initiated a system of rating the quality of hybrids and species. From one to four stars indicated increasing quality; no stars denoted either a very poor sort or a hybrid too new or unexceptional to be rated. Beginning in 1950, the American Rhododendron Society (ARS) established a rating system to be based on evaluations made in the United States. Expressed either as numerals or corresponding numbers of plus marks, the ratings are **5**–Superior; **4**–Above average; **3**–Average; **2**–Below average; **1**–Poor.

Using the number system, a variety may be rated as to both flower and plant quality, with the first number representing flower quality. Thus a rating of 5/3 tells you the bloom is "Superior" on a plant of "Average" attractiveness.

Hardiness ratings. Disappointed by discrepancies between several British hardiness ratings and the performance in this country of the rated hybrids, the ARS set out to reevaluate hybrid and species temperature tolerances. The new ratings are still undergoing some modification as species and hybrids are subjected to unusual conditions. When reading the published hardiness ratings, remember that local conditions (especially in hilly and mountainous areas) may vary considerably; gardens at lower elevations usually experience lower temperatures. The timing of low temperatures can also determine a plant's sensitivity to cold: cold spells that follow warm weather or that strike after growth has started can damage a plant even though temperatures stay within the plant's rated hardiness.

Season of bloom. The following abbreviations are used in the listings to indicate season of bloom: **VE**—Very early; **E**—Early; **EM**—Early-mid season; **M**—Mid season; **ML**—Mid season-late; **L**—Late.

These bloom seasons are of course relative to your climate. In milder climates bloom may extend over 5 months, to earliest varieties flowering in February and the latest in June. In colder parts of "rhododendron country," the bloom season will be shorter and will begin later.

Plant size at maturity

> Dwarf—under 1½ feet
> Semi-dwarf—under 3 feet
> Low—under 4½ feet
> Medium—under 6 feet
> Tall—over 6 feet

A few special terms

The botanical world has its own unique dictionary of terms—words that take on special meanings when used in connection with plants and words especially coined for talking about plants. Here are some terms that you'll encounter in the descriptive listings.

Group (or grex). A name assigned to all seedlings from a cross between two particular rhododendrons rather than to a superior individual hybrid from the cross. Seedlings of that cross produced by anyone, anywhere, are entitled to the group name (e.g., the 'Loderi' group), abbreviated "g." in charts. To distinguish one superior seedling in a group from others, individual names may be assigned (e.g., Loderi 'King George', Loderi 'Venus').

Hybrid. Any rhododendron that has resulted from cross-fertilization of two other rhododendrons. Hybrids may have been planned or produced by a hybridizer or may have occurred spontaneously in the wild (in the latter case, they're usually called "natural hybrids").

Indumentum. The hairy coating on the undersides of leaves of some rhododendrons. The color of indumentum can be an important decorative feature of the plant.

Series. The separation of the genus *Rhododendron* into units of closely related species (see page 7).

Truss. The flower cluster of a rhododendron.

RHODODENDRONS (White)

Name	Hardy to	Season of Bloom	Height	Rating	Characteristics
Beauty of Littleworth	−5°F/−21°C	M	Tall	4/3	White flowers speckled with red purple on upper petals; 4 to 5 inches across. Conical truss, dark green leaves. Vigorous, upright spreading.
Belle Heller	−10°F/−23°C	M	Medium	4/3	Globular trusses contain 4-inch blossoms, each marked with a conspicuous gold blotch. Handsome dark green foliage on a compact, sun-tolerant plant.
Boule de Neige	−25°F/−32°C	M	Low	3/4	Pure white flowers appear in snowball-like trusses. Light green 6-inch leaves cover a rounded plant. Susceptible to Lace Wing Fly if planted in full sun.
Catalgla	−25°F/−32°C	ML	Medium	4/2	White flowers in tall trusses. Dark green foliage, open plant. A selection of the white form of *R. catawbiense*.
Catawbiense Album	−25°F/−32°C	ML	Medium	3/3	Rounded trusses of blush to white flowers spotted greenish yellow. Compact, spreading plant with medium to dark green leaves.
Cilpinense g.	+5°F/−15°C	E	Semi-dwarf	4/4	Flowers are blush to white, funnel-shaped, in loose clusters. Shiny green leaves clothe a spreading plant. Very profuse bloom.
County of York	−15°F/−26°C	M	Tall	3/3	Pale chartreuse buds open to creamy white flowers with greenish throats; tall trusses. Deep green leaves are convex and long—up to 12 inches. Open plant habit.
Cunningham's White	−15°F/−26°C	ML	Semi-dwarf	2/3	Small white flowers with greenish blotch in small, upright trusses. Many flowers. Spreading, compact plant has shiny, rather dark foliage. Tough and adaptable.
Dora Amateis	−15°F/−26°C	EM	Semi-dwarf	4/4	White, green-spotted 2-inch flowers in clusters of three to five blooms. Rounded, compact shrub with boat-shaped leaves to 3 inches long. Vigorous.
Else Frye	+15°F/−9°C	E	Medium	4/3	A hybrid from the Maddenii series with deeply veined leaves on a rather sparce, pliable plant. Intensely fragrant flowers are white blushed pink with yellow throats.
Fragrantissimum	+20°F/−6°C	E	Medium	4/3	Nutmeg fragrance from white funnel-shaped flowers to 4 inches across. Growth is willowy, flexible; can be used as a vine, ground cover, espalier, or shrub. Responds to pinching and pruning.
Lady Alice Fitzwilliam	+20°F/−6°C	EM	Medium	4/4	Fragrant white funnel-shaped flowers to five inches across. Very similar to Fragrantissimum, but plant is more compact and upright.
Loder's White	0°F/−18°C	M	Medium	5/5	Pink buds open to lightly frilled white flowers. Plant is compact and spreading with 6-inch bright green leaves. Free-blooming.
Madame Mason	−5°F/−21°C	M	Medium	3/3	Pure white with yellow blaze on upper petals. Trusses are compact, tall, and conical. Dark green foliage.
Mother of Pearl	0°F/−18°C	M	Tall	4/3	A sport of Pink Pearl and like it in every way but color; this one opens blush pink and fades to pure white.
Mrs. Tom H. Lowinsky	−15°F/−26°C	L	Medium	3/4	Striking contrast between the blush to white flowers and the brownish orange blotch on each. Truss is rounded; fairly compact plant is vigorous, with very dark and glossy foliage. An easy grower and tolerant of heat.
Sappho	−5°F/−21°C	M	Tall	3/2	Medium-size white flowers with conspicuous purple blotch on upper petals; compact, domed truss. Open growth habit.
Snow Cap	−5°F/−21°C	EM	Low	4/4	Wide, rather flat pure white flowers in trusses of up to seven. The 3-inch leaves are flat and somewhat down-hanging, with a chalky cast to their undersides.
White Pearl	+5°F/−15°C	M	Tall	3/3	Blush flowers from pink buds fade to pure white with green centers; very large domed trusses. Very vigorous plant with 7-inch dark green leaves. Sometimes sold as Halopeanum.
Windbeam	−25°F/−32°C	EM	Semi-dwarf	4/3	White flowers change to soft pink as they age. Lavish bloomer. Small, aromatic foliage on spreading plant.

RHODODENDRONS (Pink)

Name	Hardy to	Season of Bloom	Height	Rating	Characteristics
Alice	−5°F/−21°C	M	Medium	3/4	Large deep pink to light rose flowers in large upright trusses. Vigorous, easy-to-grow plant.
Anna Rose Whitney	+5°F/−15°C	ML	Tall	4/3	Rose pink flowers to 4 inches wide in trusses of 12. Dull olive leaves. Needs room.
Antoon van Welie	−5°F/−21°C	M	Tall	3/3	Large in every way: broad, waxy 6-inch leaves and tall trusses of very large flowers of a deep, even pink. Vigorous and compact plant.
Betty Wormald	−5°F/−21°C	M	Medium	4/3	Pink, pale-centered flowers heavily spotted on upper petals, very large and flat. Huge dome-shaped truss.
Bow Bells g.	0°F/−18°C	M	Low	3/4	Pink cup-shaped flowers appear in loose trusses of up to seven. Rounded, spreading plant is well clothed in medium green, rounded leaves. New foliage is bronze.

Name	Hardy to	Season of Bloom	Height	Rating	Characteristics
Bric-a-brac g.	+5°F/−15°C	VE	Semi-dwarf	4/4	Oval 1¼-inch fuzzy leaves densely cover a spreading, graceful plant. Trusses have few flowers of light pink and white.
Cadis	−15°F/−26°C	ML	Medium	4/3	Fragrant large light pink flowers are produced in large flat trusses. Dense foliage. Needs some sun for best bloom production.
Conewago g.	−25°F/−32°C	E	Low	3/2	Small lavender-tinged pink flowers and small foliage on a vigorous, rather open plant.
Cotton Candy	0°F/−18°C	M	Tall	4/4	Spectacular display of very large soft pink blossoms in tall trusses on a robust plant with thick, dark 6-inch leaves. Takes considerable sun.
Countess of Derby	−5°F/−21°C	ML	Medium	4/3	Deep pink flowers with reddish spotting on upper petals fade to pale pink. Large, rounded truss. Open, spreading plant. Also sold as Eureka Maid.
Cynthia	−10°F/−23°C	M	Tall	3/3	Dark rose fading to lighter pink; 3-inch flowers in conical trusses. Medium to dark green foliage. Plant is compact in sun, more open in shade.
Everestianum	−15°F/−26°C	ML	Tall	2/3	Slightly bluish pink with yellow spots in the throat, frilled 2-inch flowers come in rounded trusses of 15. Dark green 5-inch leaves cover a vigorous, rounded plant. Rugged and adaptable.
Faggetter's Favourite	0°F/−18°C	M	Tall	5/4	Fragrant pink-flushed flowers with throat speckled bronze. Dark green 7-inch leaves are carried on a vigorous, upright, spreading plant. Sensitive to hot sun.
Hardijzer's Beauty	−5°F/−21°C	EM	Semi-dwarf	4/4	An "azaleadendron' from R. racemosum and a Kurume azalea. Pure light pink blooms are profuse and azalealike. Plant is vigorous, sun-tolerant.
Janet Blair	−15°F/−26°C	ML	Tall	4/3	Broad ruffled flowers are light mauve pink with golden brown blotch on upper petals, carried in tall trusses. Healthy plant is well furnished with oval 4¼-inch dark leaves.
Jock g.	−5°F/−21°C	EM	Low	2/4	Bell-shaped dark pink flowers are 3 inches across in trusses of six to eight. Dark green leaves cover a dense, spreading plant. Best growth in sun.
Lady Rosebery g.	+5°F/−15°C	M	Medium	4/3	Unusual trumpet-shaped flowers are about 2½ inches long, in pink shades, carried in fairly pendant trusses of four to six blooms. Plant is slender, upright, and willowy, with oval 3-inch leaves. Needs shelter.
Lem's Cameo	+5°F/−15°C	M	Medium	5/3	Artful blending of luminous pink, cream, and apricot, each flower is nearly 4 inches across, in domed trusses of up to 20. Deep glossy green 5-inch leaves from bronzy new growth.
Loderi g.	0°F/−18°C	M	Tall	5/4	Outstanding group of hybrids in white, blush, or pink; 32 are registered, with Loderi King George the best known. Very large trusses of large, fragrant flowers; leaves up to 8 inches long. Open plant habit. Need protection from wind and sun.
Marinus Koster	−10°F/−23°C	M	Tall	4/3	Flowers are 5 inches across, pink with brown spotting; dome-shaped truss of 10 to 12. Shiny dark green 7-inch leaves.
Mrs. C.B. van Nes	+5°F/−15°C	EM	Medium	2/2	Almost red buds open to dark pink flowers which fade rapidly to light pink; tall trusses. Fairly open plant with light green leaves.
Mrs. Charles E. Pearson	−5°F/−21°C	M	Tall	4/4	Large blush pink and orchid flowers have brown spots on upper petals; large dome-shaped trusses. Vigorous plant with dark green foliage.
Mrs. E. C. Stirling	−5°F/−21°C	M	Tall	4/4	Frilled blush pink flowers with long, decorative stamens; tall conical truss. Leaves are medium to light green on an upright, spreading plant.
Mrs. Furnival	−10°F/−23°C	ML	Medium	5/5	Clear pink flowers with light brown blotch in upper petals; tight dome-shaped trusses. Compact plant.
Mrs. G.W. Leak	+5°F/−15°C	EM	Tall	4/4	Deep pink with brown flare on upper petals; large conical trusses. Dull grayish olive leaves. Sometimes sold as Cottage Gardens Pride.
Naomi g.	−10°F/−23°C	M	Tall	4/4	Outstanding group of hybrids, 10 of which have been named. Most are rather iridescent pink with shadings of yellow, lilac, or red.
Pink Cameo	−20°F/−29°C	EM	Medium	3/3	Health and hardiness are featured in this compact, dense plant. Conical trusses carry flesh pink flowers with darker yellowish pink blotches.
Pink Pearl	−5°F/−21°C	M	Tall	3/3	Rose pink fading to blush in large, tall trusses. Open, rangy growth without some shaping. A very dependable grower and bloomer.
Pink Twins	−15°F/−26°C	ML	Medium	4/3	Dome-shaped trusses contain about 15 flowers of hose-in-hose formation in shrimp pink. Compact, spreading plant has broadly oval 6-inch leaves, grows slowly.
Pioneer	−20°F/−29°C	E	Medium	2/3	Light pink flowers 1 inch across, freely produced. Small leaves are replaced by new each spring. Upright.
P.J.M. g.	−25°F/−32°C	E	Low	3/4	The foliage is as much a feature as the flowers. Rounded medium green 1½-inch leaves turn mahogany during winter. Small trusses of light pinkish lavender blooms appear with the winter foliage. Neat and compact plant, tolerant of heat and sun or shade.
Point Defiance	−5°F/−21°C	M	Tall	4/4	A giant in all respects. Individual flowers are cool pink shading to white in the center, carried in tall trusses on a husky, big-leafed plant.
Praecox g.	−5°F/−21°C	E	Medium	3/3	Small rosy lilac flowers in trusses of three to four. Compact and upright, with glossy leaves. Can be sheared as a hedge. Very free-flowering.
Racil	−5°F/−21°C	E	Semi-dwarf	3/2	Small appleblossom pink, funnel-shaped flowers come in clusters of three or four. A low, mounded plant that is very versatile.

Name	Hardy to	Season of Bloom	Height	Rating	Characteristics
Rainbow	0°F/−18°C	M	Tall	4/3	Each white blossom is distinctly edged in deep pink. Growth habit is upright and narrow.
Roseum Elegans	−25°F/−32°C	ML	Tall	2/4	Fairly small rosy lavender flowers are held in domed trusses. Popular as a landscape shrub in cold climates, but is also a good performer in southeastern and southwestern gardens. Vigorous.
Royal Pink	−15°F/−26°C	M	Low	4/4	Attractive, dense foliage on a compact, rounded plant makes this a first-rate shrub. Vigorous plants are heavy bloomers with clear pink flowers.
Scintillation	−10°F/−23°C	M	Medium	4/4	Large pink flowers with bronze and yellow in the throat are held in a large domed truss. Large glossy dark leaves. Plant needs some shade.
Trude Webster	−10°F/−23°C	M	Medium	5/4	Clear pink dark-spotted flowers to 5 inches across form huge domed trusses in keeping with the broad 7-inch foliage. Good-looking as a shrub, spectacular in flower.
Walloper	−5°F/−21°C	M	Tall	5/4	Aptly named, with huge deep pink flowers, trusses, and foliage all in proportion. Also known as Red Walloper.

RHODODENDRONS (Red)

Name	Hardy to	Season of Bloom	Height	Rating	Characteristics
America	−25°F/−32°C	ML	Medium	2/2	Small dark red flowers in ball-shaped truss. Plant is spreading, with better shape in full sun. Dull green foliage.
Bessie Howells	−15°F/−26°C	EM	Low	2/3	Rounded trusses are packed with ruffled rosy red blossoms, each flower with a dark red blotch. Very free-flowering. Leaves are dark green, 4 inches long.
Britannia	−5°F/−21°C	ML	Medium	4/4	Crimson to scarlet flowers in rounded truss. Light dull green leaves; spreading, compact plant.
Caractacus	−25°F/−32°C	L	Medium	1/3	Purplish red flowers, excellent compact plant. Foliage may yellow in the sun.
Cary Ann	−5°F/−21°C	M	Low	3/4	Funnel-shaped coral red flowers are 2 inches across in trusses of as many as 17. Handsome foliage clothes a broad, compact plant.
Cornubia g.	+15°F/−9°C	VE	Tall	4/3	Large blood red flowers in conical trusses. Medium green leaves on a fast-growing, upright plant.
David	+5°F/−15°C	M	Tall	4/3	Dark blood red flowers with contrasting white anthers; upright, loose truss. Dark green leaves on an upright plant.
Dr. V.H. Rutgers	−15°F/−26°C	ML	Medium	2/3	Fringed aniline red flowers. Dark green leaves clothe a broad, dense plant.
Earl of Athlone	0°F/−18°C	EM	Medium	5/2	Striking bell-shaped blood red flowers come in compact domed trusses. Open, spreading plant with dark green leaves.
Elizabeth g.	0°F/−18°C	EM	Low	4/4	Trumpet-shaped red flowers 3½ inches wide, in clusters of six to eight. Dark green leaves on compact, mounded plant. Very free bloomer.
Etta Burrows	5°F/−15°C	E	Medium	4/4	Dark narrow 9-inch leaves set off the brilliant blood red 3-inch blossoms that come in trusses of up to 30 flowers.
Fireman Jeff	0°F/−18°C	M	Low	5/4	Bright hot red flowers, each with a red calyx nearly as large as the petals; about 10 flowers in each rounded truss. Compact plant with elliptical medium green foliage.
Grierosplendour g.	0°F/−18°C	ML	Low	3/3	Plum colored flowers in a medium-size rounded truss. Plant is upright when young but becomes rounded and spreading when mature. Young plants bloom profusely.
Grosclaude g.	+5°F/−15°C	ML	Low	4/4	Tubular or bell-shaped waxy red flowers in trusses of 9 to 12. Leaves are dark green with brown indumentum. Slow growth.
Halfdan Lem	−5°F/−21°C	M	Medium	5/4	Bright red 3½-inch flowers come in tight trusses of about a dozen blossoms. Vigorous plant is covered with broad 8-inch dark green leaves.
Holden	−15°F/−26°C	M	Medium	3/4	Rose red flowers with darker red eye come in rounded trusses. Large dark green leaves, compact plant.
Ignatius Sargent	−25°F/−32°C	ML	Medium	2/2	Slightly fragrant large rose red flowers. Large leaves, open plant.
Kluis Sensation	0°F/−18°C	ML	Medium	3/2	Dark red flowers produced in small tight trusses. Leaves are dark green and crinkled. Compact plant.
Lady Bligh	0°F/−18°C	M	Medium	4/3	Strawberry red 3-inch flowers fade to pink with white centers; 10 to 12 in a rounded truss. Leaves are medium green on a spreading plant.
Leo g.	−5°F/−21°C	M	Medium	5/3	Waxy cranberry red flowers in full dome-shaped trusses of 20 to 24. Dark green leaves to 7 inches cover a dome-shaped plant.
Mars	−10°F/−23°C	ML	Low to Medium	4/3	Deep red blooms with contrasting light stamens; compact, high truss. Plant is slow-growing and compact, with dark green leaves.

Name	Hardy to	Season of Bloom	Height	Rating	Characteristics
May Day g.	+5°F/−15°C	EM	Low	4/3	Bright scarlet trumpets are held in lax trusses to a plant that eventually becomes broader than high. Leaves are 3 to 4 inches long with tan indumentum.
Nova Zembla	−20°F/−29°C	M	Medium	3/3	Dark red with deeper spots on upper petals. Polished dark leaves, round flower trusses. Good plant habit, adaptable over much of United States.
Noyo Chief	+5°F/−15°C	M	Medium	4/5	Foliage is an outstanding feature: highly polished, deeply ribbed, dark green. Ruffled rosy red 2½-inch flowers come in compact rounded trusses.
President Roosevelt	0°F/−18°C	EM	Medium	4/5	Ruffled flowers are cherry red merging to white centers, in compact and rounded trusses. But the foliage makes the difference: each leaf is variously marked with yellow.
Ruby Bowman	0°F/−18°C	M	Medium	4/4	Rose red with red throat, the wavy 4½-inch flowers come in domed trusses of 13 to 15. Light green leaves, up to 8 inches, clothe the rounded plant to the ground.
Scarlet Wonder	−15°F/−26°C	M	Semi-dwarf	5/5	The plant would be an excellent shrub even if it never flowered: very compact, densely covered with glossy textured leaves. Bright red ruffled flowers come profusely in flattened trusses.
Taurus	−5°F/−21°C	EM	Tall	4/4	Robust is the word for Taurus. Ball-shaped trusses carry up to 16 ruffled bright red funnel-shaped blossoms—against broadly elliptical 7-inch leaves. Plant is full and full-foliaged.
The Hon. Jean Marie de Montague	0°F/−18°C	M	Medium	3/4	Brilliant red flowers in rounded trusses. Attractive dark green foliage. Compact.
Trilby	−5°F/−21°C	ML	Medium	3/3	Dark red blooms with blackish center in ball-shaped truss. Large leaves are gray to olive green, on compact plant.
Unknown Warrior	+5°F/−15°C	E	Medium	3/2	Light red 3-inch flowers in domed trusses. Flowers need sun protection but plant is leggy in shade. Upright, open plant; early training pays off. Dark green 6-inch leaves. Good in warm climate.

RHODODENDRONS (Yellow Shades)

Name	Hardy to	Season of Bloom	Height	Rating	Characteristics
Autumn Gold	−5°F/−21°C	ML	Medium	4/3	Wide, rounded flowers are orange salmon with pink tints and orange centers, carried in rounded trusses. Dense foliage is medium green. Tolerates heat, but flowers are best with some shade.
Broughtonii Aureum	0°F/−18°C	ML	Low	3/2	A rhododendron-azalea hybrid. Soft yellow flowers with orange spots appear in small rounded trusses. Leaves are thin, 4 inches long, and semideciduous. Plant is sprawling, better where summers are warm. A good southern California plant.
Butterfly	0°F/−18°C	M	Medium	3/3	Large light yellow flowers spotted red in throat; compact truss. Grows well in sun.
Carita g.	+5°F/−15°C	EM	Medium	4/4	Light yellow blooms in trusses of 12 to 13, domed to flat-topped. Needs sun protection; shy bloomer when young. Several named clones are sold.
C.I.S.	+10°F/−12°C	M	Medium	4/2	Funnel-shaped 4-inch flowers are orange yellow with brilliant red throat; loose medium-size trusses. Undulating 6-inch leaves. Must have light shade.
Cowslip g.	0°F/−18°C	E	Low	3/2	Bell-shaped flowers of primrose to cream, flushed pink. Plant is low and mounded with oval leaves less than 3 inches long.
Crest	−5°F/−21°C	ML	Tall	5/3	Large trusses of 12 yellow flowers, each 4 inches wide. Glossy oval leaves are held for one year only.
Devonshire Cream	0°F/−18°C	M	Semi-dwarf	3/4	Creamy yellow flowers with a red basal blotch come in ball-shaped compact trusses. Dark green 2-inch leaves. Plant is very slow growing and compact.
Fabia g.	+10°F/−12°C	M	Low	3/3	A number of named clones from this group are sold; most are in shades of orange, but colors range from pink to vermillion. Lax trusses. Plants are compact, leaves have reddish brown indumentum.
Full Moon	−5°F/−21°C	M	Medium	4/3	Waxy rich yellow flowers to 3½ inches wide, in rounded trusses of about 10 blossoms. Foliage is glossy with distinct veins. Best with some shade.
Goldfort	−10°F/−23°C	M	Tall	4/3	Light yellow flowers with pink and green tints; medium-size rounded trusses. Upright and open plant.
Harvest Moon	0°F/−18°C	M	Medium	3/3	Pale lemon 3½-inch flowers are lightly spotted red; trusses are rounded and compact. Shiny yellow green leaves; upright plant.
Hotei	+5°F/−15°C	M	Low	4/3	Compact plant with medium green oval leaves is backdrop for beautiful canary yellow, ruffled, broadly cup-shaped flowers.
Idealist g.	+5°F/−15°C	EM	Medium	4/3	Wide bell-shaped pale yellow flowers are tinted green, in trusses of 10 to 12. Medium to dark green leaves; upright plant. Needs some shade.
King of Shrubs	+5°F/−15°C	ML	Medium	4/2	Apricot yellow blooms with rose shadings; lax trusses display the large flowers. Open plant with light green leaves grows wider than tall. Prefers afternoon shade.

Name	Hardy to	Season of Bloom	Height	Rating	Characteristics
Moonstone g.	−5°F/−21°C	E	Semi-dwarf	4/4	Bell-shaped creamy yellow flowers open pink, in lax trusses of three to five. Leaves are oval, flat, and medium green, about 2½ inches long. Compact, mounded plant prefers afternoon shade.
Mrs. Betty Robertson	+5°F/−15°C	M	Low	3/3	Pale yellow blooms spotted red on upper petals; medium-size flowers are carried in compact dome-shaped truss. Dark leaves, compact shrub that prefers some shade.
Odee Wright	−5°F/−21°C	M	Low	4/4	Peach buds open to waxy cool yellow blossoms, up to 15 in each truss. Plant is compact, with thick-textured dark green oval leaves.
Shamrock	−5°F/−21°C	EM	Dwarf	4/4	From a very compact, spreading plant come trusses of azalealike chartreuse flowers about 1½ inches wide. A fine and unusual foreground or rock garden plant.
Souvenir of W.C. Slocock	−5°F/−21°C	M	Low	3/3	Tight conical trusses of apricot flowers that change to light yellow. Medium green 4-inch leaves; compact, upright, but spreading plant. Slow growth.
Unique	+5°F/−15°C	EM	Low	3/5	Red buds open to pale yellow flowers flushed peach, in dome-shaped trusses. A first-class landscape shrub; neat, symmetrical, and compact, with 3-inch oval leaves.
Yellow Hammer	+10°F/−12°C	EM	Medium	4/3	Very small leaves and flowers. Blooms are bright yellow, in clusters of three; leaves are light green. Will take full sun.

RHODODENDRONS (Blue and Purple)

Name	Hardy to	Season of Bloom	Height	Rating	Characteristics
A. Bedford	−5°F/−21°C	ML	Tall	4/3	Warm blue with dark blotch on upper petal. Flowers 3¼ inches across in dome-shaped truss. Tall, vigorous plant.
Anah Kruschke	−10°F/−23°C	L	Medium	2/3	Lavender blue flowers in large, tight, conical trusses. Compact plant with dark green foliage. Does well in sun.
Barto Blue	+5°F/−15°C	EM	Tall	4/3	Fine blue color; trusses of three flowers face outward. Tall, upright plant. Leaves to 3 inches.
Bluebird g.	0°F/−18°C	EM	Semi-dwarf	5/3	Many small blue flowers on a compact, spreading plant. Leaves less than 2 inches long. Best in sunny location.
Blue Diamond g.	0°F/−18°C	EM	Low	5/4	Profuse intense blue flowers on upright, compact plant. Leaves about 1 inch long. Best in sunny spot.
Blue Ensign	−10°F/−23°C	M	Medium	4/4	Lavender blue with black spot, six to nine flowers in a rounded truss. Glossy dark green leaves; upright, spreading plant that tolerates sun.
Blue Jay	−5°F/−21°C	ML	Medium	4/3	Lavender blue flowers with brown blotch; compact, conical truss. Compact plant with large bright green leaves.
Blue Peter	−10°F/−23°C	M	Medium	4/3	Frilled lavender blue flowers with purple blotch; conical truss. Spreads wider than high, takes sun.
Blue Tit g.	0°F/−18°C	EM	Semi-dwarf	4/4	Small light blue to grayish blue flowers cover a compact, low plant. Dense green 1 inch leaves.
Caroline	−15°F/−26°C	ML	Tall	3/3	Fragrant orchid lavender flowers are especially long-lasting. Long waxy leaves have wavy margins.
Fastuosum Plenum	−10°F/−23°C	ML	Tall	3/3	Semi-double 2-inch flowers are lavender blue, in full trusses. Leaves are dull dark green above, light green below. Plant takes full sun but flowers need part shade. Vigorous.
Lee's Dark Purple	−5°F/−21°C	ML	Medium	None	Large trusses of dark purple flowers are held against dark wavy foliage. Good in Southwest.
Marchioness of Lansdowne	−15°F/−26°C	L	Medium	3/3	Light rose violet flowers with blackish blotches come in tight dome-shaped trusses. Somewhat open, spreading plant.
Parsons Gloriosum	−25°F/−32°C	ML	Medium	2/2	Lavender flowers with pink shadings; truss is compact and conical. Dark leaves, compact plant.
Purple Splendour	−10°F/−23°C	ML	Medium	4/3	Considered the finest dark purple, ruffled with a black blotch on upper petals. Compact.
Ramapo	−25°F/−32°C	EM	Dwarf	4/4	Bright light violet small flowers are in pleasing contrast to the small grayish green foliage. Plant is neat, spreading but compact.
Russautinii g.	−5°F/−21°C	EM	Medium	4/3	Blue to purplish 1-inch flowers are freely produced on an upright shrub. Leaves are medium green, 1 inch long.
Sapphire	0°F/−18°C	EM	Dwarf	4/4	Small azalealike flowers of a bright light blue. Small aromatic leaves have slight bluish cast. Spreading and dense in sun, taller and more open in shade.
Van Nes Sensation	0°F/−18°C	M	Medium	3/4	Fragrant, pale lilac shading to a white center, 4 inches across; very large domed truss. Spreading plant of medium compactness.

Rhododendron hybrids and Kurume azalea

RHODODENDRON VERSATILITY

The magnificence of blossoming rhododendrons may be featured in several ways. A single container plant is an automatic standout. You can prolong a display of color by planting varieties that have different bloom periods. Or feature rhododendrons in the company of other plants with similar cultural needs: azaleas, Japanese maples, ferns.

Rhododendron yakusimanum

Crest

BEAUTIES FROM THE WILD

Rhododendron enthusiasts have long known that excellent ornamental plants can be discovered in the wild: beautiful species untouched by hybridization. Some fine species forms have been taken directly from the wild; others have been selected from among plants of a given species that were raised from seed. The photos here show not only fine forms of various species but also part of the great range of flower and foliage types among rhododendrons.

Rhododendron yakusimanum

Rhododendron zoelleri

Rhododendron racemosum

Rhododendron orbiculare

Catawbiense Album

Rhododendron augustinii 'Electra'

OLD FAVORITES

Just because a variety is old doesn't mean it's obsolete or no longer worth growing. Some of the most beautiful and satisfactory—hence most popular—rhododendrons are veterans. Most of the ones illustrated here were introduced before 1900; 'Cynthia' and 'Sappho' have been grown for over 100 years.

Blue Peter

Mrs. Furnival

Sappho

Purple Splendour

Anah Kruschke

Cynthia

Pink Pearl

RECENT FAVORITES AND RISING STARS

New hybrids come, and many of them go—or at least find lasting popularity only in the gardens of rhododendron specialists. But some recent introductions show promise of becoming the old favorites of tomorrow. Here are a few of the candidates.

Shamrock

Halfdan Lem

Taurus

Trude Webster

Odee Wright

Point Defiance

Noyo Chief

Walloper

Lem's Cameo

Etta Burrows

Full Moon

Hotei

Snow Cap

Fireman Jeff

Dora Amateis

CHOICE PLANTS FOR SMALLER GARDENS

Without doubt, some of the most impressive rhododendrons are the old garage-size specimen plants that are annually smothered in bloom. But many contemporary homes can't accommodate such mammoth shrubs. The varieties shown here should remain in the five-feet-and-under range.

Elizabeth

Bow Bells

C.I.S.

Scarlet Wonder

Unique

May Day

THE BIG SPLASH

If you think of rhododendrons as large, you won't be disappointed by the varieties illustrated here. These are among the most popular varieties that are suitable for parks, estates, and large home gardens.

Belle Heller

Naomi 'Nautilus'

Mrs. G. W. Leak

Janet Blair

Autumn Gold

Loderi 'King George'

RHODODENDRONS THAT DARE TO BE DIFFERENT

As further illustration of the point that rhododendrons can be more than "big and pink," here are five departures from the usual: variegated foliage, patterned flowers, pendant blossoms, one specimen that could pass for a lavender azalea, and one—'Hardijzer's Beauty'—that's actually a hybrid between a rhododendron and a Kurume azalea.

Rainbow

Lady Rosebery

President Roosevelt

Hardijzer's Beauty

Blue Diamond

Classic camellias
Bountiful camellias are pillars of the winter
and early spring landscape. Largest plants
here are *Camellia reticulata* varieties.

Camellias

A gift from the Orient to temperate gardens of the world, camellias have long held a position of esteem in their native lands. In China, Japan, and Korea, the camellia motif is a familiar decoration on everything from architecture to textiles.

Though precise dates are difficult to establish, it is certain that one species, *Camellia sinensis*, was grown extensively in China at least 2,000 years before Christ—not for the beauty of its flowers but for its leaves, which were used to make tea. A thousand years later, from eastern Asia come references to camellia blossoms as adornments at festive occasions and as symbolic of particular virtues. Even the seeds were put to use, as a source of oil.

By A.D. 800, when Charlemagne had consolidated central Europe into what would be known for 1,000 years as the Holy Roman Empire, there were on record in China descriptions of 72 different forms of *Camellia reticulata*.

From Asia to the West

The photographs on pages 89–96 reveal not only the beauty of these flowers that enchanted the inhabitants of their native lands but also the great range of colors, sizes, floral forms, and styles. That such treasures should reach other parts of the world, there to be cultivated and enjoyed, was only a matter of time.

Arrival in Europe

How the first camellias reached Europe is no mystery: they came by ship. But precisely when and to what country is unclear. It is probable, though not documented, that the first *Camellia japonica* plants arrived in Portugal in the mid to late 1500s. That they were introduced in England in the early 1700s is a matter of record. It is also certain that *C. japonica*, the most familiar camellia of gardens, was described and named by the Swedish botanist Linnaeus in 1735. The name *camellia* commemorates Georg Joseph Kamel (1661–1707), a Moravian Jesuit who worked in the Philippines as a pharmacist, physician, and botanist—and who probably never saw a camellia.

But for modern gardeners, the history of camellias really begins in 1792, when a ship of the British East India Company carried to England a camellia designated 'Alba Plena'. Even now, nearly 200 years after its introduction to the West, 'Alba Plena' remains one of the most popular and widely available *C. japonica* varieties. How old it actually is can only be conjectured; Chinese horticulture has a history of several thousand years!

65

19th century development

'Alba Plena' was in the vanguard of the many old Chinese garden varieties of *C. japonica* that would be imported from China; a few others ('Donckelarii', for example) are still in the nursery trade. The first *C. reticulata*, 'Captain Rawes', reached England in 1820. When they were introduced to the European gardening public, the Chinese garden names of the camellias were changed (and often Latinized) to make them more euphonious to the European ear.

Soon after the earliest imports flowered, enterprising European nurseries started raising new varieties from seed. Italy may have led other countries in the production of new varieties during the 19th century, but many also came from France, Belgium, Germany, England, and Portugal. By the end of the century, hundreds of named varieties of *C. japonica* had been offered for sale.

The opening of Japan. Though Japan's horticultural history is less ancient than that of China, it is likely that *C. japonica* was being grown and selected as a garden ornament in Japan as far back as the 1400s. But during the 18th and early 19th century heydey of horticultural importing from the Far East, Japan was virtually closed to trade with European nations. Not until this commercial isolation was ended by treaty in 1859 were the riches of Japanese horticulture made available to an ever-widening gardening public.

Introduced on all three continents, the Japanese *C. japonica* garden varieties of camellia often left behind their lovely, sometimes centuries-old original names. Thus 'Usu-Otome' became 'Pink Perfection' in California and was introduced in Germany as 'Frau Minna Seidel'. Similarly, the old favorite 'Herme' came to Germany originally as 'Hikaru-Genji'. Only a few 19th century Japanese imports such as 'Daikagura' and 'Nagasaki' managed to retain their original and colorful names.

The Various Camellias

In the eastern Asian homeland of the camellia, there are at least 80 different species. But for the general gardening public only four are of major importance: *Camellia japonica, C. reticulata, C. sasanqua,* and *C. hiemalis* (the varieties of the last are usually catalogued with the sasanquas). Camellia enthusiasts grow various other species, but the chief value of these other species lies in the hybrids they may make with the japonicas, reticulatas, and sasanquas.

Camellia japonica

Mention the word "camellia" and most people will automatically think of *Camellia japonica*. The first to enter the European horticultural world, varieties of this species have dominated the camellia nursery trade ever since.

Within this species occur all the camellia flower forms, from the simple five-petaled single to the completely double, and flowers of a wide variety of colors: purest white, all shades of pink from blush to deepest rose, light to dark red, and variegations of these colors in differing patterns. Blossom sizes range from miniatures less than 2 inches across to lush 7-inch stunners.

These camellias generally have the best-looking foliage—rich, glossy green, and abundant. Ultimately, japonicas may reach heights of 30 feet with a spread nearly equal to that. But they may take more than one person's lifetime to achieve such proportions.

Partly because of its great number of varieties, this species also embraces the longest blooming season of all camellias. Covering a period of about 6 months, the earliest varieties start to bloom in late autumn and the latest finish in late spring. A careful selection of varieties can keep your garden in flower through the leanest floral period of the year.

Camellia reticulata

The word most often associated with *Camellia reticulata* is "spectacular." In size of both flower and plant, reticulatas are the largest: blooms may reach 9 inches across, and old Chinese records speak of ancient plants 50 feet tall. The name *reticulata*—meaning "netted" or "veined"—was given to this species because the leaf veining is indented and more prominent than that of most other camellias. The species grows wild in southern and southwestern China.

Apart from their size, reticulata flowers are often distinguishable for the silky sheen of their petals as well. Colors vary from red through medium pink, some variegated with white, and newer varieties are extending the color range to lighter shades of pink and even white. Characteristically, these blossoms are semidouble with prominent stamens;

Camellia japonica

Camellia reticulata

in many varieties, some petals tend to flute and curl and stand up in "rabbit ear" fashion. A very few are fully double, rose form, or peony form.

Reticulatas are more open and treelike (some would say sparse or gaunt) than most japonicas, and reticulata foliage lacks the richness and glossiness of japonicas. Less free-flowering than japonicas, reticulatas compensate by the size of individual blossoms. As a group they are also less tolerant of cold (to about 10°F/−12°C).

'Captain Rawes', the first reticulata to leave China, reached England in 1820; a second variety, 'Pagoda' ('Robert Fortune'), arrived in 1857. The next consignment of old Chinese garden varieties went to two enthusiasts in southern California—91 years later. Since 1948 the number of varieties available has increased slowly as a few new ones were raised from seed. Numerous recent imports from China, as well as accelerated breeding, will swell the ranks in time but will be sold chiefly by nurseries specializing in camellias. A number of reticulata hybrids—most bred with japonica varieties—combine the splendor of the reticulata blossom with more attractive plant characteristics.

Camellia sasanqua

Varieties of *Camellia sasanqua* (and the closely related *C. hiemalis*) are the harbingers of camellia season. Beginning in chrysanthemum time—autumn—they are mostly finished blooming by the time the japonicas begin to take center stage.

Though the individual blossoms of most sasanquas are not as impressive or lasting as those of the reticulatas and many japonicas, sasanqua plants compensate by producing more blooms than other camellias—the sasanqua is truly the "azalea" of the camellia world. Colors include the full range of white through pink to red, and all flower forms are represented.

Versatility is the sasanqua hallmark. Their finer leaf texture and somewhat bushier character make some varieties highly desirable as hedge plants. Others are willowy growers, some almost vinelike, and can be used as ground covers in semishady lo-

cations; these can also be easily espaliered or grown in hanging containers. Sasanquas are a bit more tolerant of sun than are japonicas, but they're a little less cold tolerant. If not restrained, the more upright types of sasanquas will grow as high as 20 feet.

Other species and hybrids

Japonicas, reticulatas, and sasanquas are the camellia gardener's "big three." But there are a number of other species that, though not spectacular in themselves, can contribute to a garden as hybrids (with japonicas, reticulatas, and sasanquas).

The earliest hybrids to achieve popularity were combinations of the free-flowering *C. saluenensis* with japonica varieties and—less often—with reticulatas. The results, typified by 'J. C. Williams' and 'Donation', were rather japonicalike plants with a profusion of medium-sized pink flowers. Further and more diverse breeding has produced a larger, more varied group of hybrids notable for an abundance of flowers over a long period, for their early blooming, for their better performance in sunny locations, and for blooms that range from orchid to nearly lavender in color. In general, these hybrids are vigorous, bushy growers—attractive shrubs throughout the year.

Reticulata hybrids, which wed floral magnificence with more attractive or more useful garden plants, are becoming available in greater quantity and variety. Many are simply hybrids with japonicas, but an increasing number result from breeding reticulatas with other species or hybrids. The melting pot is only beginning to boil.

Camellias of tomorrow

Plant enthusiasts tend to be incorrigible dreamers—and among camellia enthusiasts, two dreams of long standing have been flower fragrance and yellow color. One of these has already been partly fulfilled, and the other now seems delectably possible.

Fragrance is there already in several of the less spectacular species, and some hybrids have been

Camellia sasanqua

produced that combine fragrance with improved flowers. Persistent hybridizing should, in time, add distinct fragrance to the striking blossoms of japonicas and even reticulatas.

Yellow-flowered camellia species, known for years, have remained frustratingly out of reach for breeders: they are native to strife-torn and politically inaccessible northern Indochina. But the year 1980, when the first plants of the yellow *C. chrysantha* were raised from seed in the United States, may have marked a turning point in camellia development. The new species already seems promising for its foliage alone, which has the gloss of japonica, veining more pronounced than reticulata, and size apparently greater than either. Here's the unanswered question: will the new species cross easily with japonicas and reticulatas, and if so, will the hybrids be immediately fertile? The process may be slow, but imagination runs rampant. Imagine japonica-style plants and flowers—not only in yellow but also in shades of apricot, coral, orange, bronze, and purple!

Camellias in the Landscape

Even if camellias never flowered, most would rank high on any list of recommended landscape shrubs. But as they are, capable of sending forth beautiful blossoms during the months when garden color is at low ebb, camellias rise above the category of "recommended"—even approaching that of "essential" for some aficionados. Only climate limits their use, and as noted under "Special Accommodations" (pages 80–82), the effects of climate can be modified or circumvented by gardeners in less-than-favorable regions who are captivated by camellia's charms.

The descriptions of principal species and hybrids on pages 66–67 points up the diversity of flowers, flowering times, foliage, and plant habits at the gardener's disposal; the account of their native habitat (pages 68–69) outlines the conditions they prefer. With this information in mind, consider the various landscaping possibilities camellias offer.

Woodland garden. The gardener lucky enough to have dappled shade from tall trees can use camellias as nature distributed them in the forests of eastern Asia. Casually grouped around meandering paths under high shade according to color, size, type, and bloom season, camellias can help you achieve a fusion of natural beauty and artistic control.

Basic shrubbery. The idea may seem dull, but think of the need in every garden for basic shrubbery, and then reflect on the virtues of using camellias for such plantings. Whether along a fence or walkway, against house walls, or as a backdrop to lower shrubs, perennials, or annuals, camellias can give a landscape dignity and polish throughout the year, punctuated by colorful blossoms in their season.

Accent specimen. Visualize just one camellia plant in full flower; then imagine it placed in partly shaded garden area that you'd like highlighted during the year's least colorful period. A camellia could greet you beside your front door or welcome you at the garden entrance. A tubbed specimen might become the focal point of an intimate patio, or a large japonica or tall reticulata under high shade could be a garden beacon in a picture-window view.

Trained as espaliers, camellias can lend both foliage and floral beauty to walls and fences where shade or space restrictions rule out other—and less attractive—choices. Among the sasanquas are some of such pliable growth that you can consider them almost as vines.

Container plants. Camellias take so well to container culture that many gardeners actually prefer growing them that way. When growing them in containers, you have greater control over water and nutrients, and you always have the option of moving plants to a more favorable or more conspicuous location. More details and advantages of container culture are covered on pages 80–82.

Hedges. Many sasanquas, many hybrids, and some japonicas are both vigorous and dense enough to be massed in line as hedge and barrier plantings. They'll look their best when only lightly clipped— just enough to remove straggling growth—rather than formally sheared; they'll also produce more blooms.

Ground covers. The more willowy or vinelike sasanquas can easily be coaxed into service as ground cover plantings. All year they'll offer handsome, polished foliage, and in autumn they'll nearly smother themselves with blossoms.

The Wheres and Hows of Planting

Camellia culture is not difficult, provided you know the plants' specific needs for healthy growth. But a list of "do's and don'ts" won't give you as full an understanding of those needs as will knowledge of the camellia in its native habitat. Fortified with such knowledge, you can achieve success by duplicating the natural conditions as closely as possible in your garden.

The native environment

Imagine yourself standing on a hillside in a semitropical forest where the lush vegetation is open rather than impenetrable. Surrounding you are a variety of handsome plants, from a few feet to more than 20 feet high, some of which you recognize as wild rhododendrons and azaleas not yet ready to burst into bloom. Included in this forest undergrowth are specimens of one especially attractive shrub—neater than the others, with foliage that appears polished. At the moment they are in full bloom—it seems with as many flowers as leaves. Some are bright red, some pink, others white, while still others show variegations of these colors. Closer inspection reveals that some of these shrubs are really 30-foot trees with trunks a foot thick. These plants are, of course, wild camellias.

Beneath your feet is a thick, soft carpet of decaying leaves and twigs. You brush aside some of this natural mulch and examine the soil beneath: it's loose, crumbly, perhaps even a bit gravelly—and moist. You can squeeze a handful of it into a compact ball, but when you drop the lump of soil to the ground it will crumble.

Next you are aware of the atmosphere. A wind comes up—brisk in the treetops but more moderate below—bringing rain. The shower is heavy but its force is broken by the canopy of trees, while the abundant moisture that reaches the forest floor is quickly absorbed by the natural mulch and the humus-rich, porous soil. Such showers are frequent but brief. The clouds depart and the sun returns—filtered, of course, by the trees—leaving behind freshened air, washed leaves, and moist soil.

Such a scene can be found nearly anywhere in natural camellia country, a roughly S-shaped region that extends from the subtropical mountainous valleys in southwestern China and northern Indochina up the China coast, covering Taiwan and other islands, to its northernmost limits in Korea and Japan. Though it's a temperate zone, variations in the severity of the winter cold throughout the camellia range affect the hardiness of various species and hybrids. During the growing season, the whole territory receives generous rainfall.

The general description of the camellia's native habitat highlights most of their essential needs. In summary, they are these:
- *Protection* from extremes of sunshine and wind.
- *Soil* that is well drained (evidenced by its loose and crumbly texture and by the location of plants on hillsides, where any excess of water drains away downslope) and well fortified with organic matter (through the continual decay of natural mulch). In regions where rainfall is high and lots of organic matter continuously decomposes, the soil is typically acid. Thus camellias thrive in a soil that is slightly on the acid side of neutral. (For details on soils and planting, see pages 68–75.)
- *Moisture* to ensure soil that is continuously moist but never soggy (remember the importance of

good drainage); also frequent moistening of foliage from rainfall or overhead watering.

Fortified with an understanding of their natural preferences, you can evaluate your garden's suitability for camellias. But don't despair if your garden at first appears inhospitable; refer to the section on "Special Accommodations" (pages 80–82), where you'll find advice on how to circumvent such handicaps as poor drainage, alkaline soil, lack of shelter from winter cold, and too much sun.

Selecting a planting site

Camellias are not plants for total, dense shade. Under such conditions they may seem to grow well enough, but it will be at the expense of their compactness and bloom production. As suggested in the description of their native habitat, these plants need sunlight that is modified or diluted from full intensity.

Just how much modification will depend on your climate. In the fog belt of the West Coast, camellias will often thrive in garden locations that receive full sun; relatively cool high temperatures, infrequent sunny days, and constant humidity make for conditions that camellias like even in full-sun locations.

On the other hand, where summers are hot and dry, it is essential to filter overhead sunlight to modify its intensity and retard loss of water from soil and through leaves. In the absence of trees, you can put up overhead structures that will accomplish the same purpose (see "Climate modification," page 82). Or you can plant camellias where they will be shaded by a house, wall, or fence during the hottest hours of a summer day—along an east-facing wall, for example, where the plants will get sun during the cooler morning hours but will be in shade during the afternoon heat. Even normally hot exposures—south and west—can provide homes for camellias if there are trees or buildings that will filter or block the sun's rays during the heat of the day. North-facing exposures that receive little or no direct sunlight will prove congenial as long as the light is not further reduced by heavy shading from trees or adjacent buildings.

Mingling with trees. If you want to plant your camellias among or under trees, choose trees that don't produce dense shade and that don't have a thick, shallow network of greedy roots that will compete with the camellias for water and nutrients. Beeches and many maples, for example, are poor companions for camellias. So are pines and most other needle-leafed evergreens, though camellias can be planted in thinned-out evergreen forests if placed far enough away from trees to avoid competition from their roots.

(Continued on page 71)

CAMELLIA COUNTRY

"Camellia Country"—where japonicas and sasanquas can be expected to comfortably endure a normal winter—embraces the Atlantic, Gulf, and Pacific coasts of the United States, extending northward and inland as far as winter temperatures don't drop below 10°F/−12°C.

But the camellia's survival, as explained on the facing page, depends on a complex interaction of exposure, wind, and onset of low temperatures as much as on the lowest temperature actually recorded. Roots will be severely damaged at about 20°F/−6°C (hence the need for a good winter mulch in colder regions), but many japonicas can survive 0°F/−18°C or even lower if they are well sheltered from wind and sun and the temperature drop is grad-

ual. Also, established plants are less vulnerable to damage from low temperatures than are young, recently planted ones.

If winter weather were totally predictable and regular—temperatures gradually and steadily falling during the autumn and steadily rising in the spring—it would be possible to draw a precise map of where camellias can be grown. But with the inevitable fluctuations between winter cold and warm spells, the margin of camellia country is really blurred. Success in the colder areas will depend on the weather, the gardener's knowledge and skill, and the plant itself. There are healthy, established plants in areas (around New York City, for example) that in theory should be too cold for camellias outdoors.

...Continued from page 69

When selecting sites for your camellias, remember to avoid windswept locations. Not only does wind distort plant growth and spoil flowers, it also accelerates water loss from soil and leaves, and in practical terms that means frequent watering by the gardener.

Where winters are cold. Near the outer reaches of "camellia country" (see facing page), where winter temperatures are the limiting factor, gardeners have to locate plants so as to protect them from freezing temperatures. Since cold air seeks the lowest level, plants near the top of a hillside will probably suffer less damage than those at the bottom. Plants growing beneath trees that remain green in winter (or under shelter of some sort) will be in less peril than plants exposed to open night sky, because any kind of shelter will intercept some of the heat lost from the ground at night.

Protection from drying winds is critical, as leaves may give up moisture to subfreezing winds faster than roots can replace it. The result will be a severely damaged or dead plant. In regions where the ground may freeze for extended periods, it is important to get plants well watered in advance of expected freezing and to maintain a good winter mulch to prevent or at least minimize freezing of the soil. Camellia roots are hardy only to about 20°F/ −6°C, so container-grown camellias are especially vulnerable in marginal regions.

All your efforts can be confounded by a sudden severe freeze after an autumn of warm weather. Camellias, like plants in general, will come through low temperatures better if they are conditioned by gradual cooling. A sudden freeze catches plants unprepared for their normal approach to winter, their cells usually too full of water which freezes, rupturing the cells and killing the tissues.

Because many camellias are in bud or in bloom during the coldest months, it is important to give buds and blossoms the greatest possible protection not only from freezing, but also from the damage caused when early morning sunlight strikes frozen buds and flowers. In the fringe areas of camellia culture, the plants that will stand the best chance of blooming well and regularly are those located in the warmest parts of the garden but shielded from direct early morning sunlight—and the longer the shielding, the better.

How to select a healthy plant

Whatever camellia you buy, you want to be sure to choose a healthy plant that will enter your garden with no handicaps. When choosing, you'll want to keep several criteria in mind, but the first general rule is that a good nursery is likely to offer only quality stock. If you're shopping in a shabby or run-down nursery (perhaps because it offers a wide selection of camellias), you should scrutinize the plants quite thoroughly.

When considering a plant, look at it carefully, and if there are several plants of the same variety, compare them. The leaves should be shiny, rich green (note: reticulata foliage is typically not glossy). If you're shopping in the autumn or winter months, after the new growth of that year has matured, look for leaves among the most recent growth that are as large as or larger than those from previous years; smaller new growth indicates an undernourished plant. Avoid plants with pale, yellowish, or dull leaves or new growth that is noticeably smaller than the older growth. Though yellowish foliage might simply indicate overexposure to sunlight, it—and the other characteristics just mentioned—could well be a sign of poor care and nutrition.

Steer clear of plants that seem to have been too long in their nursery containers. Look for the common tipoffs: dead stems or twigs, often on a plant that seems leggy and shows little new growth; a rusted-out metal container or a container with a low level of soil, hard-packed soil, or lots of roots showing above the soil. (With a healthy plant, don't worry about a few roots showing above soil level—as long as it's in a full container of soil.)

A vigorous-looking plant is usually supported by a good root system, but from even the best of nurseries you may sometimes get a rootbound plant—one that's been in its container so long that its roots are dense, matted, and even growing in circles around the perimeter of the root ball. Take a sharp stick or a screwdriver and try to loosen the congested roots. If they're tightly matted, take a knife and vertically score the sides of the root ball an inch or two deep in four equidistant places; then try loosening the root mass. If roots are growing in circles, try bare-rooting the plant (see page 81); be sure to plant quickly with roots spread out.

The best times to plant

Camellias are just like other shrubs in that they are best planted and transplanted when dormant, with neither roots nor leaves and stems in active growth. Unlike most other shrubs, though, camellias are dormant during their flowering period. This means that the most pleasant time to shop for camellias—when you can see the blossoms—is also a good time to plant.

The camellia's dormant period, however, is longer than its flowering season. Dormancy begins after the year's new growth has hardened (usually in late September or October) and ends shortly after the flowering period. Where there is little danger of damaging winter freezes, planting early in the dormant season gives plants the greatest opportunity to adjust to your garden before onset of spring growth. In the colder fringe areas of camellia country, though, many growers prefer to set out new plants in spring before new growth is due to begin.

Actually, you can plant camellias from containers at any other time of year if you take a few precautions. Delay planting until afternoon or early evening when the temperature is falling rather than rising, and don't set out plants during a heat wave. For at least a month after planting, temporarily shade plants from any direct sunlight; and, if the weather is very warm, lightly spray the foliage with water at least once daily. If the plant is producing soft new growth, expect some temporary wilting.

Soil preparation

In nature, a germinating camellia seed sends down a taproot that, in time, will penetrate deeply enough into the soil to sustain the plant through any unusual drought period. The main root system branches off from the taproot in the top 1 to 2 feet of soil.

Commercially grown camellias, on the other hand, are started from cuttings or grafted onto seedling plants from which the taproot was pinched in infancy. The plant you buy for your garden, then, has no taproot; it will develop a root system that will become wide-spreading in time, but not deep—a fact you'll want to take into account when preparing the soil and planting.

The earlier section on the camellia's native environment stressed the need for soil that is well drained but moisture retentive, and slightly acid. Roots need cool dampness plus ample air in the soil, while slight acidity ensures that all the nutrients needed for healthy growth will be available. The best soils for camellias, then, range from loam to sand well fortified with organic matter. (See special feature on "The Basics of Soil," page 74.)

In contrast, dense clay soils—even though they are moisture retentive—offer the least friendly home for camellia roots because the particles in such soils are so small and tightly packed that drainage is extremely slow; roots remain not just moist but saturated, and will suffocate from lack of soil air. This is especially true of level clay soils; clay soil on a slope or hillside can be more accommodating because drainage is both downward and downslope, so roots are in less danger of prolonged saturation.

You can improve the drainage and aeration of clay soils by adding copious amounts of organic matter, but here's the problem: because it will absorb water much more slowly, the clay soil around and beneath the improved soil will prevent water from draining away quickly enough. You get a "bathtub effect"—roots still suffocate, just in a better soil. Also, the roots will tend to remain within the improved soil rather than penetrate into surrounding denser material, and this, of course, will restrict plant growth. Clay soils are not hopeless, but they do call for special treatment (see page 73).

Basic planting guidelines

It has been speculated that more failures with camellias can be traced to too-deep planting than to

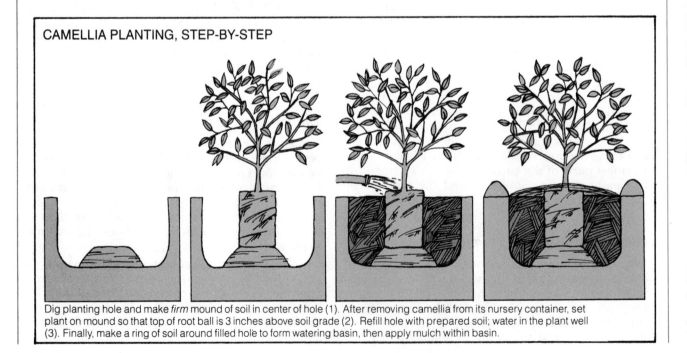

CAMELLIA PLANTING, STEP-BY-STEP

Dig planting hole and make *firm* mound of soil in center of hole (1). After removing camellia from its nursery container, set plant on mound so that top of root ball is 3 inches above soil grade (2). Refill hole with prepared soil; water in the plant well (3). Finally, make a ring of soil around filled hole to form watering basin, then apply mulch within basin.

any other single cause: the roots simply smother. Knowing this, and remembering that roots grow out rather than down, you'll understand that you need not dig a deep planting hole but a broad one.

Sand and loam soils. A planting hole 14 to 16 inches deep is sufficient—a bit more than double the depth of the root ball of a 1-gallon container plant, and just a few inches deeper than that from a 5-gallon size. Do make the hole about three times as wide as the plant's root ball.

To the soil you remove from the planting hole, thoroughly mix in a roughly equal amount of organic matter (caution: if you use peat moss, you must completely saturate it first, then squeeze out excess water, before mixing with soil). Return some of this mixture to the hole and solidly tamp it down—enough so that when placed on the tamped soil, the plant's root ball will be about 3 inches above the surrounding soil surface. Then fill in around the root ball with the remaining soil mixture and water it well. Should the root ball sink during watering, reach into the wet soil, grasp the root ball and gently raise it back to 3 inches above the surrounding soil. In time the plant will settle a bit, as organic matter in the soil decays, but the high planting will compensate.

When you finish planting, make a watering basin by forming a ridge of soil around the outside of the filled-in hole. Add a mulch (see page 75) over the soil around the plant so that the mulch *just* covers the top of the root ball. The watering basin will help keep the mulch in place.

PLANTING IN PROBLEM SITES

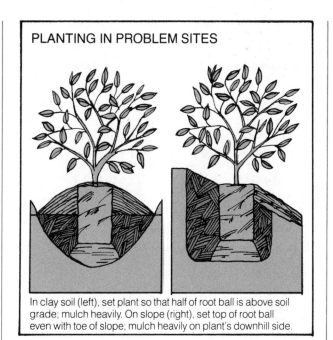

In clay soil (left), set plant so that half of root ball is above soil grade; mulch heavily. On slope (right), set top of root ball even with toe of slope; mulch heavily on plant's downhill side.

Clay soils. If you have dense clay soil, you have three options. One is to use organic matter to improve a broad, shallow, saucer-shaped hole in the clay, plant the camellia high—the top of its root ball well above the soil surface—and mulch heavily, as shown in the illustration above. The elevated planting will allow better drainage of water from the root zone.

A better procedure, particularly if you want to plant a number of camellias, is to create raised beds

TRANSPLANTING A LARGE CAMELLIA

With a sharp spade, cut a circle to spade's depth around plant to mark the size of root ball you want. Then dig trench around outside of circle to form sides of root ball. Wrap ball securely with poultry netting (if necessary, undercut ball with spade), use pick or shovel as lever to raise root ball, and lift out of hole. Replant as shown on page 72.

Camellias, azaleas, and rhododendrons all need soil that is both well drained and moist: their roots need air in the soil but should not dry out. This discussion of general soil types should give you an understanding of your garden soil; the explanation of organic matter will suggest its importance to soil quality.

Soil types

Soil consists of mineral particles, organic matter—some living, like soil bacteria, and some dead and in the process of decay—plus air and water in the pore spaces between particles. The shapes, sizes, and relative proportions of the different mineral particles determine the *type* of soil; the quantity of organic matter influences a soil's *quality.* Soils, then, are almost infinitely variable. Nevertheless, gardeners speak of three general types—clay, sand, and loam.

Clay soil consists of microscopically small mineral particles that are flat and packed closely together, somewhat like a deck of cards. The pore spaces between particles are correspondingly small, making it difficult for water and air to penetrate. Clay soils are called heavy or poorly drained because the downward movement of water is very slow, but when thoroughly moistened these soils are slow to dry out. Roots have the greatest difficulty growing and spreading in tightly knit clay soils. On the positive side, clay soils tend to be rich in nutrients; and because drainage is slow, the dissolved nutrients in the soil are not quickly leached away.

Sandy soils represent the other extreme. The mineral particles are large (from 5 to over 100 times larger than the largest clay particles) and rounded rather than flat. Sand particles fit together much more loosely than clay particles, leaving substantially larger pore spaces between. Roots penetrate sandy soils easily. Water penetrates easily, too, but also drains out more rapidly. Therefore, plants in sandy soils need watering more frequently than those in clay, and such watering leaches out nutrients faster.

Loam is the term used to describe a soil type that contains a mixture of particle sizes: clay, sand, and an intermediate-size particle called silt. Its capacity for retaining nutrients and water is between that of clay and that of sand; the same is true for the size of its pore spaces. Root growth is not hindered in loam as it is in clay. Add organic matter to loam and you get what is often referred to as "good garden soil."

Organic matter

Organic matter is a general term for a broad range of materials—mainly the decomposing remains of plants. It is the dark, crumbly debris of decaying leaves on a forest floor; the compost deliberately made by gardeners; agricultural by-products such as apple and grape pomace or rice hulls, sawdust, or wood chips; and a variety of packaged materials available at nurseries and garden centers, such as peat moss, ground bark, and mixtures labeled "garden compost" or "forest humus."

Incorporated into lighter, sandier soils, organic matter lodges in the relatively large pore spaces between soil particles, acting as a "sponge" to retain water and dissolved nutrients. In denser, more clay-like soils, organic matter helps improve aeration and drainage by separating the small, tightly compressed soil particles.

Any given volume of organic matter will, in time, decay totally; the matter will be consumed by soil organisms, and the resulting nutrients will be shared by organisms and plant roots. Thus it's important to incorporate fresh organic matter into soil at planting time to create a soil structure that will give roots the best possible start in their new garden environment. Thereafter, maintaining a mulch (see page 75) will provide material for decomposition and will keep the top several inches of soil crumbly and porous, so that water and feeder roots can move through it easily.

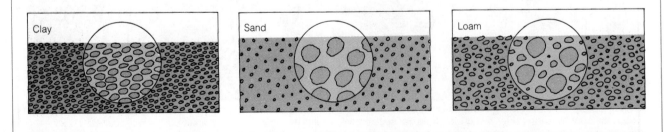

for planting, filling the beds with a mixture of soil and organic matter that will be more to the roots' liking.

The third possibility is to plant in containers. Raised beds and container planting are discussed under "Special Accommodations" on pages 80–82.

Camellia Care and Keeping

Careful planting, as outlined on pages 68–75, will start your camellias on a potentially long and happy life in your garden. But to ensure that they'll flourish, you'll need to know what routine attentions they'll need, and when. Proper care is especially important during the first 3 to 5 years after planting. The camellia is basically a tough shrub or tree *once it is well established*. Venerable plants in old neighborhoods demonstrate this, growing happily with little water, without mulch, and sometimes in full sun. But you can bet that such husky survivors were well cared for in their youth, when they established far-reaching root systems and a large leaf canopy to shade the root zone in lieu of a mulch.

Watering

The time of year, climate, planting location, soil, and size of your camellias will affect how often you have to water them. Sandy soils will lose water more rapidly than loam soils. Whatever the soil, it will retain moisture longer in shaded locations than in more sunny ones. Wind and heat both draw moisture from leaves, and thus from the soil. And a young plant with a small root system will need more careful watching than will an established plant.

The important point is that camellias need a soil that is moist—but not soggy—throughout the year. They're not deep-rooted plants, but you should be sure that the entire root zone is moistened when you water. Rainfall, especially in the summer, is a great boon to camellia foliage, but don't assume that it will always supply the roots' needs. Check the soil. Use your fingers, a trowel, a pointed stick, or a soil auger to determine how deeply any watering has penetrated.

How to water. Roots *need* water, and foliage appreciates it. Your primary objective, then, is to keep the entire root zone moist. You can do this by irrigating, with basins around each plant; by using low sprinklers to cover the ground beneath the plants; or by using sprinklers mounted high enough to water the plants as well, in the manner of rainfall.

In parts of California and the Southwest, water may contain various salts that in time will harm camellias. Leaves may show marginal burn or exhibit chlorosis (see page 79) where there's such a buildup of alkalinity in the soil. Chlorosis can be counteracted fairly simply; but where accumulated salts hamper plant growth, the only solution is periodic flushing out of the salts from the soil (called *leaching*). This is usually difficult and impractical for plants growing in the ground. Where salt buildup is a hazard, camellias are best grown in raised beds or containers from which accumulated salts can be leached more easily. Do this by thoroughly irrigating a raised bed for several hours; flood a container for 5 to 15 minutes—the longer time for larger containers. Leaching every 6 months, just before the onset of new growth and again half a year later, should be sufficient.

Overhead watering isn't a "must" where the humidity is high; but where the air is dry, it can be very beneficial, especially during the warmest months. It washes the leaves and slows the transpiration of water from them. In regions with very dry summers, a daily syringing isn't too much.

Mulching

It's impossible to discuss watering without bringing up the subject of mulches and mulching. Simply stated, a mulch is a layer of organic matter (in nature, a layer of fallen leaves) on top of the soil. It keeps the soil both cooler and more moist than soil exposed to sun and air, and prevents the soil from becoming muddy when wet and caked when dry.

In their native habitat (see page 68), camellias benefit from a carpet of decaying leaves and twigs on the forest floor. So take a cue from nature and provide a mulch beneath your plants.

In choosing a mulch, you'll have a wide selection, probably limited only by availability and cost. The best mulches are those that don't pack down tightly, thus allowing easy penetration of water. High on the list are pine needles and oak leaves. If you make you own compost, the partly decayed larger pieces are good for mulching. You may be able to buy ground bark, bark chips, or wood chips, either packaged or by the truckload, from your municipal parks department. Agricultural by-products such as ground corncobs, spent mushroom compost, and grape pomace are useful as mulches.

Sold nearly everywhere, peat moss has been used as a mulch, but you must understand its idiosyncrasies. Peat moss is usually dry when you buy it, and you must soak it thoroughly before using it as mulch. Knead handfuls of it in a bucket of water so that the fibers are completely saturated, and squeeze out all the excess water. Then you can apply it. As long as you water consistently, the peat moss will function well as a mulch. But if you let it dry out completely, it can be blown away by the wind, and what remains on the ground may actually repel water.

Other widely available materials that make mulches include animal manures (as long as they are well rotted rather than fresh), straw, and hay. Even lawn clippings can be used if you either let them dry before applying them or apply them in thin layers, letting each layer dry before applying the next. Piled on thickly while still green, grass clippings will become slimy and compact as they try to decompose, repelling water rather than letting it through.

Nutrients and fertilizers

In the wild, camellias get their nutrients only from the decaying organic matter beneath them—with, no doubt, the occasional gift of nitrogen from bird droppings. Many successful camellia growers follow nature's example and rely on a continuously decaying mulch to provide all necessary nutrients. But there are other equally successful growers who use commercial fertilizers to lend nature a hand. The choice is yours—be guided by the performance of your plants. The sandier and more fast-draining your soil, the more likely that you'll want to use some sort of fertilizer.

If you choose to supply additional nutrients, use one of the commercial fertilizers specially formulated for camellias (usually labeled as camellia, azalea, and rhododendron food or simply as acid fertilizer), or use cottonseed meal. The directions on packaged camellia fertilizer will tell you how much to use, based on the size of your plants. The first application should be made at the start of the bloom season, followed by another just before the onset of new growth.

Some growers advocate further applications—at 6 to 8-week intervals throughout the summer. But this is likely to stimulate a second flush of growth that will be vulnerable to frost damage in colder regions and that may also interfere with flower bud development—or at least obscure the blossoms during the next bloom season.

Cottonseed meal is a slow-acting organic fertilizer that can be applied just at the onset of bloom and twice thereafter at 1-month intervals.

Be sure that the soil is moist when you apply any fertilizer, and water it well immediately after application. If you're in any doubt about how much fertilizer to use, be conservative. Too many camellias have been damaged or even killed by overzealous gardeners using a heavy hand when applying fertilizers.

During a plant's first year in your garden, let the roots establish themselves with only routine watering and mulching. If you feel the urge to add nutrients thereafter, go cautiously during the next 2 or 3 years: use only half the recommended amount for each application.

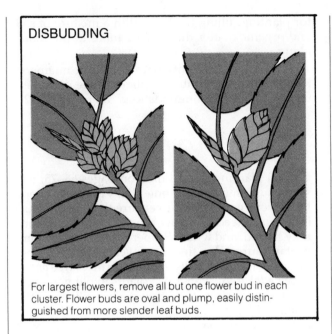

DISBUDDING

For largest flowers, remove all but one flower bud in each cluster. Flower buds are oval and plump, easily distinguished from more slender leaf buds.

Disbudding

Disbudding is not exactly "routine care." Most camellias will produce more than one flower bud at each point on a stem where buds form, and in some varieties there may be three to six in each cluster. The result will be plenty of color but smaller individual flowers. Growers who aim for the largest possible flowers will disbud their plants regularly, while many home gardeners prefer a greater quantity of flowers to larger individual blossoms.

Some varieties often develop more buds than they can mature properly and will drop a number of buds before bloom season, effectively eliminating any need for manual disbudding. Hard freezes can also perform the task of disbudding—sometimes totally. But if your plants are in good health, some natural disbudding is no cause for alarm.

By late summer, you'll be able to distinguish the plump, oval flower buds from the long, slender growth buds in the same cluster. If you decide to disbud, leave one or two flower buds at the end of each branch and, moving back on the stem, leave one flower bud every 3 to 4 inches. Spare flower buds of different sizes; the smaller ones will mature later and prolong the bloom season. To remove a bud, grasp it firmly and gently *twist* it off. If you try to pull or break it off, you may accidentally remove the growth bud as well.

Pruning

Unlike other flowering shrubs—many roses, for example—camellias need no annual pruning to stay healthy and attractive. Many beautiful old bushes have never been touched by pruning shears except,

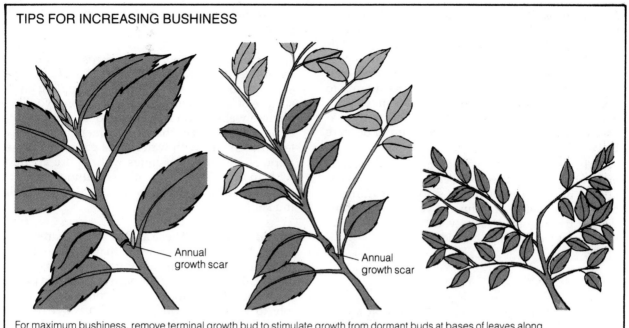

TIPS FOR INCREASING BUSHINESS

Annual growth scar

Annual growth scar

For maximum bushiness, remove terminal growth bud to stimulate growth from dormant buds at bases of leaves along stem. Or cut out last year's growth to the annual growth scar; several branches will start below cut.

at most, for the cutting of blossoms for the house. But it would be misleading to suggest that camellias will not benefit from some pruning, shaping, or guiding.

The illustrations on this page show the kinds of pruning cuts you may make. Here we discuss the four reasons for considering pruning.

Compactness. Some varieties will tend to grow horizontally more than vertically in their youth. To encourage more upright growth, you may have to cut back some of the spreading branches to keep growth energies from being expended in the undesired direction. This is no guarantee that vertical growth will speed up, but the plant will at least be more compact and dense as it edges its way upward.

Bushiness. Some camellias, notably the reticulatas, are naturally rangy, leggy, or open in growth habit. Some are sparsely branched, and others grow such long stems in a season that the branches are far apart. You can't alter any plant's natural inclination, but you can fatten up such plants by removing growth buds before they start into growth or by removing the entire length of last year's growth. Either procedure forces several dormant growth buds to grow below the removed portion; random cutting, on the other hand, usually stimulates only the growth bud immediately below each cut.

Thinning. Older bushes may carry a number of twigs that are alive but not producing flowers (or

that are producing flowers of poor quality). These twigs are often found toward the inside of the plant, where they are starved for light and will, in time, simply die. Removing such superfluous twiggy growth will reserve the plant's energies for the remaining healthy growth.

Some varieties of camellia have such dense growth that they can profit from thinning simply to open up the plants a bit for better flower display. With these, the growth you remove will include not only the twiggy and unproductive kind, but also some that is healthy and vigorous. In most thinning operations, you'll be cutting back entire branches to older, leafless wood in order to let light in.

Training. Many of the sasanquas are almost vinelike and can be used as shrubby ground covers. The same sasanquas and some japonicas with spreading or willowy growth habits can be trained as espaliers against a wall or fence. The most vigorous japonicas and many reticulatas can in time be coaxed into treelike shapes if not into actual trees.

Each type of training involves removing growth that departs from the desired form or tying it into place. For ground covers, trim away any branches that grow straight up. For espaliers, remove branches that grow straight out from the wall or fence. A plant designed to become a tree will need its lower branches removed in order to develop a smooth trunk. And any camellia in any situation may need occasional shaping; remove the stems or branches that depart from the overall shape of the plant as you want it to be.

Rejuvenation. What do you do with the 12-foot camellia that's blocking the dining room window? Transplant? Maybe, but it's a chore. Or consider cutting it back—*way* back. Though the result may at first resemble a pruned rosebush, you can expect it to put forth plenty of new growth in its attempt to rebuild. After the first year, you can thin out unwanted or unnecessary shoots—removing, for example, those that would only grow up to obscure the window again.

The best time for any major pruning is near the end of the dormant season, before new growth has begun. But you can do minor snipping, cutting, or branch removal at any time of year. If you prune during the bloom season, you can get some cut flowers for the house as a dividend.

Plant Problems

Camellia growers are fortunate that so lovely a plant is so little bothered by pests or diseases. In fact, most camellia failures can be traced to poor cultural practices—which suggests that the camellia's number one problem is the gardener!

This is not to say that a camellia will not be visited by a few pests and diseases, but few will assault it in such force as to warrant attempts at control. Described below are the most common "unwanted visitors" and the measures needed to control them, should you find it necessary.

Pests

Plant pests—creatures that crawl around—fall into two general categories: those that suck the plant's juices and those that chew. Here in order of frequency, are the four most likely to be found on camellias.

Scale insects (sucking). Camellias may be host to any of several types of scale insects. Though color and size will vary according to type, all scale insects live inside stationary waxy shells that adhere to a leaf or stem. Because of the waxy shells, ordinary contact insecticides usually fail to reach and destroy the insects.

Oil spray can kill scale insects by smothering them; the insecticide malathion added to the oil spray will be most effective, as the oil will carry the insecticide through the protective covering. But oil sprays must be used with caution: oil can damage camellias if the temperature goes above 85°F/29°C or falls below 40°F/4°C soon after application. Oil sprays are safest in spring and autumn.

For year-round use, systemic insecticides such as cygon and orthene give effective control. With these insecticides, plants absorb the toxic ingredi-ent so that sucking insects die from ingesting the plant juices.

Spider mites (sucking). These microscopic pests are warm-weather creatures. The first sign of their presence is usually a yellowish or pale stippling on the surface of leaves; with heavy infestations, you'll see a white webbing on leaf undersides. Light infestations may be kept in check by frequent hosing-off of leaf undersides with water. But heavy, established populations of spider mites will require attention with an insecticide. Systemics (see under "Scale insects") are also effective, as are insecticides containing kelthane.

Aphids (sucking). These are the familiar green, red, or black soft-bodied crawlers that can heavily colonize new growth on many garden plants. Fortunately, they are among the easiest of garden pests to eliminate. The simplest way to control them is simply to wash them off plants with water from the hose. If that fails, you can spray with a low-toxicity insecticide containing pyrethrin as the active ingredient.

Brachyrhinus beetles (chewing). In the Pacific Northwest and parts of northern California, these beetles—known as strawberry root weevils—and their larvae may pose a twofold problem. The beetles emerge only at night in spring and chew leaf edges, making characteristic square-cornered notches. Then in late summer they lay their eggs in the soil; and after hatching, the larvae burrow down and feed on tender roots. Controlling these pests is not easy, but the best bets are the insecticides sevin and diazinon or the systemic orthene. Used as a soil drench, they may control the larvae; as a foliage spray during spring and summer, they may be effective against the beetles.

Other pests. Camellia foliage may now and then tempt various other garden pests, including cucumber beetles (diabrotica), various caterpillars and worms (such as measuring worms and leaf rollers), earwigs, grasshoppers, and even snails and slugs. But seldom do these appear in such numbers as to require control—other than, perhaps, hand-picking.

Diseases

Camellias may be affected by several diseases, but only two are of major importance. One destroys the floral display, and the other inflicts its damage on the plant.

Petal blight. The disheartening blight fungus, *Sclerotinia camelliae*, can occur wherever camellias are grown, though by no means does it infect every garden. To understand why it occurs and how to combat it, you need to know its life cycle.

In an infected garden, the first sign of petal blight will be small brown specks on flower petals. The specks are formed by airborne spores of the fungus which germinate on the petals, sending threadlike filaments through the flower tissue. As the disease progresses, the flower turns brown and dies, ultimately falling to the ground. The fungus continues to grow on the fallen flower, soon forming small black bodies called sclerotia at the flower's base. These sclerotia are the second phase of the fungus's life cycle, allowing it to live through the spring, summer, and autumn.

Then during the following bloom season, when temperatures reach 50–70°F/10–21°C and enough humidity is present, small disclike cups called apothecia appear on the sclerotia. From the apothecia are formed thousands of spores that are released into the wind. Spores that find open flowers will cause infection and repeat the cycle. There is no spread of the fungus from flower to flower; it is entirely from the airborne spores infecting individual blossoms.

No chemical control is completely effective against petal blight. But you can control it by interrupting its life cycle: remove and destroy infected blossoms, the source of next year's trouble. Remove both the dead flowers that have fallen to the ground and all flowers still on the plant that show infection. Burn these blooms, bury them well, or seal them tightly in plastic bags to go out with the trash.

Two or three years of such cleaning up may be necessary before you gain control over petal blight. Some fastidious growers also remove all the mulch beneath their plants after the bloom season, discard it far away from the garden or burn it, and replace it with fresh. Others simply add a new layer of mulch over the old. If you begin flower removal at the first sure sign of infection, that alone should be sufficient. But remember that spores are carried by the wind. If other gardens in your neighborhood are infected and uncontrolled, you can anticipate some infection every year from those sources.

Dieback. Contagious dieback, caused by the fungus *Glomerella cingulata*, is found chiefly in the warm, humid Gulf Coast South at the time of new growth in the spring. Camellia varieties differ in their susceptibility to it—from the apparently immune 'Professor Charles S. Sargent' to the highly susceptible 'Ville de Nantes'. The disease does not affect the entire plant. Instead, an individual shoot among young growth will suddenly wilt and die, and in a month or two a canker will develop at the base of the dead shoot. In the canker will form spores that will be a source of infection the following year.

Spread through water and by insects, conta-

gious dieback can infect a plant only through open wounds. The time of spring growth is also the time when camellias normally shed their oldest leaves, so the leaf scars where old leaves have dropped off become a principal point of infection.

To control dieback, remove affected stems promptly. Cut the stems off and burn them or dispose of them far from the garden. Make each cut below the dead portion, into a healthy part of the stem, to remove the point where the canker would form. The systemic fungicide benomyl can control dieback fungus if you spray plants at 2-week intervals, beginning at the onset of leaf fall and continuing for about 2 months.

Leaf gall. Unsightly rather than debilitating, this fungus problem is found in the South, principally on sasanquas. Symptoms are puffy, fleshy, malformed leaves. The best means of control is to remove infected leaves and burn them.

Virus variegation. Technically, this is a disease for which there is no cure, but it's not harmful. Affected plants grow and bloom well despite the virus. The characteristic virus variegation is in shades of yellow to cream, flecked or blotchy. In contrast, genetic variegation is caused by a lack of chlorophyll in part or all of a leaf, and the contrast is usually of white to green.

Environmentally induced problems

The following symptoms result from growing conditions that, in one way or another, are not quite right for the plant.

Yellowish leaves. A camellia's leaves have about a 3-year life span, after which they naturally turn yellowish and fall from the plant—chiefly in the spring. But if the leaves on an entire plant are light green or yellowish, the plant may not be getting enough water, it may lack nutrients, or it may be in poorly drained soil. Investigate the possibility of poor drainage first; if that doesn't seem to be the cause, check your watering and fertilizing habits. If only one branch has pale yellow or white leaves, it's just an aberrant twig that lacks chlorophyll and you can leave it on the plant as a curiosity; if the leaves become sunburned, though, you might prefer to cut away the stem.

Yellow leaves with green veins. This is an iron deficiency called *chlorosis*. Where soils are acid or neutral, iron is available to plant roots. But as soil becomes alkaline, the iron is chemically "locked up" in insoluble compounds. Where soils or water tend to be alkaline, the use of acid fertilizers such as those labeled "camellia food" will help to lower the alkalinity in the camellia's root zone. If chlorosis appears, the quickest remedy is to apply iron chelate—a product that keeps iron in a soluble form available to roots. If chlorosis is a persistent problem with camellias growing in the ground, try planting them in containers or raised beds (see pages 80–82) so that you'll have greater control over the acidity of the soil.

Leaf burn. Browned leaf edges indicate injury from salts—either fertilizer salts (a result of overfertilization) or alkaline salts that have built up in the soil. The short-term remedy is to leach the salts from the plant's root zone with a long, deep watering if the plant is in the ground, or with a thorough flushing of the soil if the plant is in a container or raised bed. To prevent further leaf burn, correct the problem. If you were overfertilizing, be less generous in the future. If there's been a natural buildup of salts in the soil, consider digging up the plant and replanting in a raised bed or container.

A browned patch on the face of a leaf indicates sunburn. The plant may be in a location that's too sunny; consider moving the plant if the burn is serious and persistent.

Leaf scurf. Elongated, corky scabs on leaf undersides are signs of leaf scurf. This problem can usually be traced to overwatering or irregular watering: the roots absorb more water than the leaves can transpire, so blisters develop on the leaves. When the blisters burst, they harden into scabs. Camellias with large root systems and sparse foliage are the most susceptible, particularly the reticulatas.

Bud drop. Some varieties of camellia naturally set many flower buds and then drop some of them before they mature. This is just a natural thinning process. Some varieties may drop many—even most—of their flower buds, though the plants are growing vigorously, in a climate where they're poorly adapted for flowering. Extreme weather—an unseasonable hot spell; a sudden hard freeze; or a sudden freeze followed by bright, warm sunshine—can trigger a bud drop of alarming proportions, and there's nothing you can do. But if you have a variety that consistently fails to bloom because of bud drop, replace it with another camellia variety.

If bud drop is a constant problem, review your cultural practices. Some possible causes are too little water, erratic watering, or poor drainage.

Browned petals. If you can eliminate petal blight as the cause of browning (see page 78), sun or wind may be the problem. Either one will usually brown the edges of petals. White and pale pink blossoms are especially susceptible to sun and wind damage.

Special Accommodations

Considering its requirements for good growth (see page 69), the camellia is a remarkably adaptable plant. You needn't have just the right soil, exposure, or even climate to grow camellias well; all you need to do is "accommodate" them by creating a congenial environment.

Containers

Camellias are one of the best plants for long-term residence in containers—whether you want just one or two as special accent plantings or a large and portable collection.

In fact, portability can be a distinct advantage, no matter how many or few you grow, if you're growing camellias where the summer or winter is inhospitable. Where summers are hot and dry but winters mild, container camellias can spend the summer under shelter but be brought out to exposed patios or decks for enjoyment during the bloom season. Where winters are too cold for their outdoor survival, container camellias can spend summers outdoors but be taken to a cool "camellia house" or unheated solarium for winter display.

Choosing a container. Your choice of container is wide open, dictated by appearance rather than material. Wood tubs or planters, terra cotta pots (glazed or unglazed), plastic or metal cans—all may be satisfactory as long as they have good drainage. Water should be able to flow freely from the container immediately after watering.

A container's size is more important than what it's made of. Select a container that is no more than 4 inches greater in diameter than the camellia's root ball and no more than 1½ times its depth, to a maximum depth of about 16 inches. Soil unoccupied by roots retains water longer than does soil with roots that are actively using the water. Soggy, unoccupied soil in a container is an invitation to water mold fungi that can attack roots, weakening and eventually killing the plant.

Container soils and planting. In containers, more camellia failures can be traced to poor drainage than to any other cause—all the more reason to give special attention to the soil mixture. And unfortunately, regular garden soil—even if camellias do well in it—can't simply be scooped up and put into a container with any hope for success. Without alteration, garden soil in a container compacts into a soggy lump when wet and a bricklike mass when dry.

A good potting soil for camellias will contain 50 percent solid particles and 50 percent pore space; half the pore space will be occupied by water, the other half by air. In other words, water and air must move freely though the soil. Camellia growers have experimented with many mixes and have found several that work well. The important criteria are that the mixture drain well and that it not compact.

Here are some examples of successful container mixture formulas:

- Equal parts leaf mold, peat moss, and sandy soil.
- Equal parts peat moss, well-rotted steer manure or wood shavings, and builder's sand.
- Equal parts peat moss, ground bark, and sandy soil, and ½ part builder's sand.
- One part sandy loam soil, ½ part peat moss, ½ part leaf mold, ½ part well-rotted steer manure, and ½ part builder's sand.
- One part ground bark, 1 part leaf mold, and 2 parts builder's sand.
- Two parts ground bark, 1 part peat moss, and 1 part builder's sand.

When you decide to plant a camellia in a container, check its root ball to determine what sort of soil mixture it's in. If it appears to be porous and lightweight, similar to what you're going to place it in, you can proceed with planting. But should the soil of the root ball appear dense and heavy—like garden soil—you should *carefully* remove as much of it as possible. One way is to tap the root ball gently, knocking off as much soil as you can without breaking or tearing the roots.

Some camellia enthusiasts go so far as bare-root planting, immersing the root ball in a bucket of water to remove the soil. Whatever course you follow, it is important to replant as quickly as possible so that roots are not long exposed to drying air.

Put enough of your prepared soil mixture into the container so that the top of the root ball (or of the root system when bare-root planting) is about 1½ inches below the rim of the container. Fill in around the roots with more soil mixture, firming it lightly with your fingers, and water the plant thoroughly until water flows freely from the drainage holes.

Fertilizing container camellias. In a fast-draining container soil mixture, nutrients are leached out of a plant's root zone more quickly than from a plant in the ground. Container camellias, then, don't need more fertilizer than plants in the ground, but they need more frequent applications. The amount applied each time should be on the conservative side of what any label recommends, because the roots of container plants are vulnerable to fertilizer burn.

The favorite fertilizers for container camellias are the same as for plants in the ground: packaged "camellia food" and cottonseed meal. Slow-release fertilizers that release nutrients steadily over a period of months are also gaining in popularity.

With any kind of fertilizer, make the first application early in the flowering season. If you use "camellia food" or cottonseed meal, go light on the recommended dosage and repeat at monthly intervals until summer. The slow-release types usually supply enough nutrients for the season from just one application. Liquid fertilizers, especially those formulated for acid-loving plants, are popular with some growers because the nutrients are available immediately to plants. With liquids, also, there's no

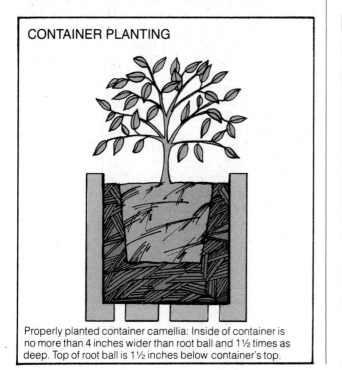

CONTAINER PLANTING

Properly planted container camellia: Inside of container is no more than 4 inches wider than root ball and 1½ times as deep. Top of root ball is 1½ inches below container's top.

ROOT-PRUNING A CONTAINER PLANT

To repot in same container, remove plant from container and trim off the outer inch of root ball with a sharp knife. Return plant to container and fill in with fresh potting mixture.

danger of root burn as long as they're diluted according to directions. Follow label directions for frequency of application, too.

Repotting. Camellias grown in containers will need periodic repotting. Smaller, young plants may need it every other year as their roots and tops grow vigorously; older, medium-size plants may go 3 to 4 years between operations.

There are two reasons for repotting. First, of course, plants tend to outgrow their container space and need larger quarters for continuing healthy growth. But container soil also tends to compact in time, as the organic matter decomposes, cutting down on drainage; the remedy is to renew at least part of the soil in the container by repotting. When shifting a plant to a larger container, remember that the new quarters should be no more than 4 inches greater in diameter than the root ball. Do your repotting at the time of year best for planting in your area (see "The best times to plant," page 71).

Large, mature camellias can remain happily in 16-inch square tubs or half barrels for years on end, needing only periodic removal (about every 4 or 5 years) for root pruning. This entails removing the camellia from its container, taking a sharp knife and cutting off the outer inch of root mass from the root ball, returning the plant to its container, and filling in with new container soil mix. The best time of year for root pruning is early autumn, after new growth has hardened and the plant has entered dormancy.

Raised beds

The raised bed is one sure way to circumvent a dense or compacted clay garden soil. Even if your soil is ideal, a raised bed can make an attractive landscape addition. A planter alongside an elevated deck, for example, will raise plants to the deck's "ground level." A raised bed or planter may define a walkway, provide separation between parts of the landscape, or stand out as a patio feature.

For use over an inhospitable clay soil, make the planting depth of a raised bed 18 to 24 inches; the camellia roots will depend entirely on the soil in this bed for their root zone. Prepare one of the planting mixtures recommended for container culture (see page 81), fill in the raised bed, and water the mix thoroughly. It will settle a little, so expect to add more and water again before you're ready to plant.

If your soil ranges from sandy to loam—basically good enough to improve for camellias (see "Soil preparation" on page 72)—you won't need such a deep raised bed; the native soil can be amended to fill out the total recommended planting depth. Amply fortified with organic matter, such soils can also be used in the raised bed.

You can make raised beds from a variety of materials: wood (decay-resistant, such as redwood or cedar), brick, concrete block, or various other construction blocks. But whatever the material, *be sure* to provide a drainage or "weep" hole at ground level every 1 or 2 feet.

Climate modification: Heat and cold

Hot summers or freezing winters present challenges to camellia growers, but as obstacles they aren't insurmountable.

Sun shelter. If you run out of walls facing north and east and your garden lacks trees, how can you accommodate more camellias? Grow them under artificial shade. An overhead structure of wood lath—½-inch by 1-inch lumber, or 1 by 1—spaced 1 to 2 inches apart, will provide the same sort of dappled shade as trees that would take years to grow. If the cost of lumber is intimidating, you can build a simpler structure and stretch shade cloth over it to cut the sun's intensity. Nursery supply houses carry shade cloth, usually in several grades of "shadiness."

Such a structure might be an overhead for a patio, doing double duty shading both plants and people during the summer. Or you might want to project a lath overhang from the south side of the house, converting a hot spot into potential camellia territory. Or you can acknowledge that you're a camellia "nut" and build a freestanding structure in the garden just for your plants.

Cold protection. Where winters are too cold for outdoor camellia culture, and even in those parts of "camellia country" (see page 70) where damage is likely in some years, camellia enthusiasts grow their plants in greenhouses. Actually, such shelters come under two headings. One is the "camellia house" that's used only as winter quarters for plants in containers, which are moved outdoors for the spring, summer, and early autumn. These shelters may be made of glass, fiberglass, or plastic, but they needn't be elaborate. You just want to keep winter temperatures above critical lows and protect flowers from rain, sleet, or snow.

The other type of shelter is the year-round greenhouse where camellias can be grown permanently in raised beds and containers.

Neither the camellia house nor the greenhouse need be warm during the winter; you want only to keep the temperature consistently above freezing. A congenial temperature range is from about 35°F/2°C at night to around 50°F/10°C during the day. If you grow camellias in a year-round greenhouse, remember that they are plants from temperate and *sub*tropical regions, not from steaming tropical jungles. During the warm months, especially, provide plenty of ventilation to keep air fresh and moving.

CAMELLIA SHOPPING GUIDE

The charts that follow describe 134 varieties of camellias, grouped according to type: japonicas, reticulatas, sasanquas, and hybrids of various sorts. This is by no means a complete listing—there are thousands of camellia varieties—but it does include the most popular and widely available sorts. Varieties are listed alphabetically within each group; a separate column calls out the basic color.

Another column contains symbols for season of bloom.

E = Early   October to January
M = Midseason   January to March
L = Late   March to May

Where winters are coldest within camellia country, bloom usually begins in January and may continue until June. No bloom season symbol is listed for the sasanquas since nearly all of them are early bloomers. Exceptions are noted in individual descriptions.

The descriptions contain a few terms that may have special meanings when applied to camellias. *Fimbriated* means fringed; it refers to petal edges that are fringed in the manner of carnations. *Stamens* are the yellow filaments—actually reproductive organs—that appear prominently in the center of many camellia flowers. *Variegated* indicates that the basic color is spotted, marbled, flecked,

striped, or otherwise marked with a second color. An asterisk (*) after a variety's name indicates that there is also a variegated form of that variety in commerce, the name of which is the same followed by the word "Variegated" (often abbreviated "Var."). On red and pink varieties, the variegation is usually of white; variegated forms of white varieties are marked with pink or red.

Notation of typical flower size (in diameter) is based on the following scale:

Miniature	2½ inches or less
Small	2½ to 3 inches
Medium	3 to 3½ inches
Medium large	3½ to 4 inches
Large	4 to 5 inches
Very large	Over 5 inches

If a variety is sometimes sold under other names, these synonyms appear immediately following the description. The correct names, as well as descriptions of flower and plant forms, are in accordance with *Camellia Nomenclature,* published by the Southern California Camellia Society, Inc., and adopted as the official nomenclature of the American Camellia Society.

Parent species of hybrids are listed in parentheses at the beginning of descriptions.

CAMELLIA FLOWER FORMS

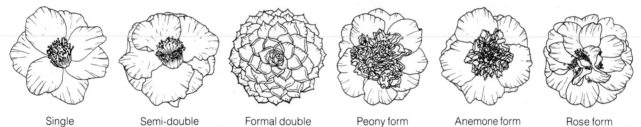

Single   Semi-double   Formal double   Peony form   Anemone form   Rose form

JAPONICAS

Name	Color	Season	Description
Adolphe Audusson*	Red	M	Dark red, large, and semidouble, with broad, wavy petals, and crown of brilliant gold stamens. Growth is medium, compact, upright. A prolific and reliable old favorite. *Synonyms:* Adolphe, Audrey Hopfer.
Adolphe Audusson Special	White and red	M	A variegated sport of Adolphe Audusson, mostly white with a few splashes of dark red. Growth and performance identical to parent plant.
Alba Plena	White	E	Pure white. Large, formal double flower with a short blooming period. Slow, bushy growth—good in containers. Protect blooms from rain.
Anita	Pink and red	M	Light pink striped with red. Medium-large, semidouble; individual flowers are short-lived. Vigorous, upright, and compact plant.
Barbara Woodroof	Pink and white	E–M	Sport of Elegans (Chandler) Var. Large, anemone-form flower with light orchid pink guard petals and white center petaloids. Slow, spreading growth.
Bernice Boddy	Pink	M	Light pink with deep pink under petals. Medium-size, semidouble flowers. Growth is vigorous and upright; performs well in coldest regions of "camellia country."

Name	Color	Season	Description
Betty Sheffield	White, red and pink	M	White, striped and blotched with red and pink. Large blossoms are semidouble to peony form with loose petals and stamens intermingled among slightly waved petals. Medium, upright growth.
Betty Sheffield Blush	Pink	M	A sport of Betty Sheffield with the same plant and flower characteristics but blooms of light pink with a few deep pink marks.
Betty Sheffield Coral	Pink	M	A sport of Betty Sheffield with the same plant and flower characteristics but blooms of solid coral pink.
Betty Sheffield Supreme	White and red	M	A sport of Betty Sheffield with the same plant and flower characteristics but blooms of white with deep rose red border on each petal.
Blood of China*	Red	L	Deep salmon red. Large, semidouble to loose peony form. Plant is vigorous and spreading but compact. Late bloom season is disadvantage in warm areas. *Synonyms:* Victor Emmanuel, Alice Slack.
Bob Hope	Red	M	Dark, brilliant red. Blooms are large to very large, semidouble with irregular petals. Growth is fairly slow, upright, compact, and bushy.
Carter's Sunburst*	Pink	E–L	Pale pink striped with deeper pink. Large to very large blooms, semidouble to peony form to formal double. Compact plant.
Clark Hubbs*	Red	M	Rich, dark red. Large blossoms, full to loose peony form with fimbriated petals. Vigorous plant is upright and compact.
C. M. Hovey*	Red	L	Dark red. Formal double flowers are medium to large; petals shatter instead of falling off altogether. Medium-size, slender, and upright plant. *Synonyms:* Colonel Firey, Wm. S. Hastie.
C. M. Wilson*	Pink	E–M	A light pink sport of Elegans (Chandler) Var. with the same large anemone-form flower and slow, spreading growth. *Synonyms:* Grace Burkhard, Lucille Ferrell.
Covina	Pink	M	Deep rose to rosy red. Small, semidouble to rose-form blossoms. Noted not for individual flowers but for profusion of them on compact, sun tolerant plant. Good for hedges.
Daikagura	Pink and white	E	Bright rose pink splashed with white. Medium to large peony-form flowers that do not fall from the plant when spent. Free-blooming; slow, compact growth. *Synonyms:* Idaten-Shibori, Kiyosu.
Debutante	Pink	E–M	Light pink. Medium to large flowers, full peony form. Plant is vigorous, upright, and bushy; tolerant of more sun than most japonicas. A heavy bloomer. *Synonym:* Sarah C. Hastie.
Donckelarii	Red and white	M	Red marbled with white, with a considerable range of variegation. Large, semidouble blossoms. Growth is slow and bushy.
Drama Girl*	Pink	M	Deep salmon rose pink. Very large, semidouble flowers with broad, wavy petals. Plant is vigorous, tall, and open, with somewhat pendulous habit.
Dr. Tinsley	Pink	M	Petals are very pale pink at bases, shading to deeper pink at edges; backs of petals are flesh pink. Medium blooms, semidouble like wild roses. Compact, upright.
Eleanor Hagood*	Pink	L	Soft, pale pink. Formal double blossoms are medium to large—beautifully regular but not always opening well. Vigorous, upright growth.
Eleanor McCown	White, red, and pink	M	White streaked with red and pink. Striking blossoms are medium-large, semidouble to anemone form. Growth is vigorous, upright, and open.
Elegans (Chandler)*	Pink	E–M	Very large anemone-form flowers have solid pink guard petals and center petaloids often spotted with white. Slow, spreading growth. *Synonyms:* Chandleri Elegans Pink, Francine.
Elegans Champagne	White	E–M	A sport of Elegans Splendor with the flower form and plant habit of the Elegans group but white flowers with cream petaloids in centers.
Elegans Splendor	Pink and white	E–M	A sport of C. M. Wilson with the flower form and plant habit of the Elegans group. Bloom is light pink edged with white, anemone form, with deep petal serrations. *Synonym:* C. M. Wilson Splendor.
Elegans Supreme	Pink	E–M	A sport of Elegans (Chandler) with the same flower form and plant habit. Bloom is rose pink with very deep petal serrations.
Fimbriata	White	E	A sport of Alba Plena with the same plant and flower characteristics, but all petals have fimbriated edges. *Synonym:* Alba Fimbriata.
Finlandia*	White	E–M	Pure white. Medium-large blooms are semidouble with swirled and fluted petals. Free-flowering; medium, compact growth. *Synonyms:* Dearest, Nellie White.
Flame*	Red	M	Deep flame red. Flowers are medium to large, semidouble. Compact, upright, vigorous growth—a durable, trouble-free old favorite.
Flowerwood*	Red	M–L	A sport of Mathotiana with the same vigorous, upright growth and large rose form to formal double crimson blossoms—except that petal edges are fimbriated. *Synonym:* Mathotiana Fimbriata.

Name	Color	Season	Description
Gigantea	Red and white	M	Deep red marbled with white—a striking contrast. Very large flowers are anemone form to semidouble or peony form. Very vigorous, upright, open plant. *Synonyms:* Emperor Wilhelm, Magnolia King, Mary Bell Glennan, Fanny Davenport, Kellingtonia, Monstruoso Rubra, Jolly Roger, Gaiety.
Glen 40*	Red	M–L	Deep red with glowing undertone. Medium to large, formal double to rose-form blossoms. Slow, compact, upright growth—a reliable favorite. *Synonym:* Coquetti.
Grand Slam*	Red	M	Dark but brilliant red. Blossoms are large to very large, semidouble or anemone form, sometimes dropping before fully open. Vigorous, open growth.
Guilio Nuccio*	Pink	M	Coral rose pink. Impressive blossoms very large, semidouble with irregular petals. A strong, upright grower.
Hawaii	Pink	E–M	A sport of C. M. Wilson with the slow, spreading growth of the Elegans group. Light pink flowers, however, are peony form wtih fimbriated petals.
Herme	Pink, and white	M	Pink petals have broad, irregular white border and occasional stripes of deeper color. Medium to large, semidouble. Upright, slender, dependable plant. *Synonyms:* Jordan's Pride, Hikaru-Genji.
High Hat	Pink	E	Light pink. A sport of Daikagura that has the same medium to large peony-form flowers on a slow, compact plant. Free-blooming.
Hi-No-Maru	Red	M	Bright red. Medium-size single flowers with conspicuous tufts of gold stamens. Slow, compact, upright growth.
Joshua E. Youtz	White	E	Pure white. Large blossoms are peony form to formal double, on a slow-growing, compact plant. Effect is that of a white Daikagura. *Synonym:* White Daikagura.
Kickoff	Pink	E–M	Pale pink petals marked with deep pink. Blossoms are large to very large, of loose peony form. Plant is vigorous, upright, and compact.
King's Ransom	Pink	M	Pale pink flowers darken as they age. Medium to large blossoms of loose peony form with broad, wavy petals. Vigorous, upright, compact growth.
Kramer's Supreme*	Red	M	Bright red with orange undertone. Large to very large flowers of peony form with petals and petaloids mixed together. Vigorous, upright; can take some sun.
Kumasaka*	Pink	M–L	Rose pink. Medium-size blossoms vary from peony form to rose form. Vigorous, compact, free-flowering. Good tolerance of both sun and cold. *Synonyms:* Lady Marion, Jeanne Kerr, Maiden, Sherbrooke, Kumasaka-Beni, Hollyhock.
Lady Kay	Red and white	M–L	A sport of Ville de Nantes with the same plant characteristics and flower color—red marked white— though flowers are loose to full peony form, fimbriated.
Lallarook	Pink and white	M–L	Rose pink, often subtly marbled with white. Medium to large blossoms are perfect formal double with recurved petal edges. Slow, compact growth. *Synonyms:* Laurel Leaf, L'Avenire.
Magnoliaeflora	Pink	M	Delicate blush pink. Medium-size, semidouble blooms resemble those of certain deciduous magnolias. Free-flowering plant of medium, compact habit. *Synonyms:* Rose of Dawn, Hagoromo, Cho-No-Hagasane.
Margaret Davis	White and red	M	Creamy white to white petals with a few rosy red lines and dashes and edged in bright red. Medium-size, peony-form blossoms. Compact, bushy plant.
Marie Bracey*	Pink	E–M	Coral rose. Blossoms are large, semidouble to loose peony form, giving a fluffy appearance. Medium-size plant is compact and upright. *Synonyms:* Spellbound, October Delight.
Masterpiece	White	M	White opening from blush pink bud. Flowers are large, formal double to rose form. Plant is vigorous, open, and upright, with very large foliage.
Mathotiana*	Red	M–L	Crimson, sometimes with purplish cast. Very large blossoms, rose form to formal double. Vigorous, compact, upright plant; good performer where summer is hot. *Synonyms:* Julia Drayton, Mathotiana Rubra, Purple Dawn, Purple Emperor, Purple Prince, William S. Hastie.
Mathotiana Supreme*	Red	M–L	A sport of Mathotiana, similar to it in all respects except that flowers are deep red, very large, and semidouble, with petals and stamens interspersed. *Synonym:* Mima-Mae.
Mrs. Charles Cobb	Red	E–M	Deep rich red. Medium to large, peony form to semidouble blossoms with large, loosely arranged petals. Vigorous, bushy plant; especially good in warmer regions.
Mrs. D. W. Davis	Pink	M	Blush pink. Very large, semidouble flowers on a strong, upright, and compact plant. A sport with peony-form flowers is Mrs. D. W. Davis Descanso.
Mrs. Tingley	Pink	M–L	Silvery soft salmon pink. The medium-size blooms are perfect formal double, freely produced on a rather tall and open plant.
Nuccio's Gem	White	E–M	Pure white. The medium to large blossoms are perfect formal double. Vigorous plant is upright and bushy.

Japonicas (cont'd.)

Name	Color	Season	Description
Nuccio's Pearl	Pink	M–L	Blush—hovering between white and pink—with center and outside petals shaded deeper pink. Medium-size, formal double blooms.
Pearl Maxwell	Pink	M–L	Soft shell pink. The medium-size blossoms are perfectly arranged formal double. Plant is compact and vigorous.
Pink Pagoda	Pink	E–M	Deep rose pink. Medium to large blossoms are formal double with wavy petals, freely produced on a vigorous, upright, and compact plant.
Pink Perfection	Pink	E–L	Delicate shell pink. Shell-like petals make up the small, formal double blossoms, which appear over a long blooming season. Vigorous, dense, upright plant; often drops many buds. *Synonyms:* Frau Minna Seidel, Usu-Otome.
Prince Eugene Napoleon	Red	M	Rosy red. Medium to large, formal double blossoms, the perfectly arranged petals becoming smaller toward blossom center. Strong, compact plant. *Synonyms:* Pope Pius IX, Imbricata Rubra Plena, Ladiner's Red.
Professor Charles S. Sargent*	Red	M	Vibrant dark red. The small to medium peony-form blossom is rounded and tightly packed with petals. A tough, easy-to-grow plant—compact and upright.
Purity	White	M–L	Pure white. Medium-size flowers vary from rose form, showing gold stamens in centers, to formal double. Plant is strong and very upright. *Synonyms:* Neige d'Oree, Shiragiku, Harriet I. Laub, Refinement, Renjo-No-Tama.
Reg Ragland*	Red	E–L	Rich red. Large blossoms are semidouble with smaller, upright center petals surrounding yellow stamens. Medium, compact growth.
Rosedale's Beauty	Red	E–L	Solid red. Medium-size rose-form flowers are plentiful. Growth is vigorous and compact, densely covered with large foliage. *Synonyms:* Mme. le Bois, Carl Rosenquist.
Shiro Chan	White	E–M	A sport of C. M. Wilson with the anemone-form flowers and slow, spreading growth of the Elegans group. Blooms are white with faint pink tinge at base.
Swan Lake	White	M–L	Large white blossoms vary from formal double to loose peony form, with yellow stamens interspersed. Thick foliage; a vigorous, upright plant.
Tiffany	Pink	M	Light orchid pink to deeper pink at petal edges. Blossoms are large to very large, loose peony form to anemone form. Strong, upright plant.
Tinsie	Red and white	M	Miniature, anemone-form flowers consist of one row of dark red guard petals and a central tuft of white petaloids. Plant is vigorous and upright.
Tomorrow*	Red	E–M	Strawberry red. Blooms are very large—semidouble with petaloids mixed in center or full peony form. Strong, open, and slightly pendulous.
Tomorrow Park Hill	Pink	E–M	A sport of Tomorrow Var. with the same plant character, but blossoms are soft, light pink deepening toward petal edges, with some white variegation.
Tomorrow's Dawn	Pink and white	E–M	A sport of Tomorrow with the same plant character but blossoms of soft, deep pink to light pink, shading to white at petal edges.
Tomorrow's Tropic Dawn	White to pink	E–M	A sport of Tomorrow's Dawn with the same plant character, but blossoms are white, occasionally streaked with red, and fade to blush as they age.
Ville de Nantes	Red and white	M–L	A sport of Donckelarii, basically identical in plant and blossom, except that all petals have fimbriated edges. Susceptible to dieback in the South.

RETICULATAS

Name	Color	Season	Description
Buddha	Pink	M	Rose pink. Very large, semidouble blossoms with irregular, wavy petals. Strong, upright growth.
Butterfly Wings	Pink	M	Rose pink. Blooms are very large, semidouble with broad, wavy petals that suggest the name. Slender, open plant.
Captain Rawes	Pink	L	Reddish rose pink. Very large, semidouble flowers with gracefully waved petals. Vigorous and bushy (for a reticulata). Probably the hardiest reticulata.
Chang's Temple	Pink	M–L	Deep rose. Large, wide open flower with deeply notched petals and some petaloids in center. Vigorous and upright.

Name	Color	Season	Description
Chrysanthemum Petal	Pink	M	Light carmine pink. The medium-size blossoms are rose form to formal double with fluted petals. Growth is slender and open.
Cornelian	Red and white	M	Rose pink to red variegated with white. Very large, semidouble to peony-form blooms have wavy, crinkled petals. Vigorous and compact. Has been sold erroneously as Chang's Temple and as Lion's Head, of which it is the variegated form.
Crimson Robe	Red	M–L	Bright red. Very large flowers with wavy, crinkled, crepe-textured petals. Plant is vigorous and spreading—better looking than most other reticulatas.
Lila Naff	Pink	M	Silvery pink. Large, semidouble blossoms with broad petals. Plant is strong, upright, and fairly compact.
Mouchang	Pink	M	Salmon pink. The very large flowers are single to semidouble, on a plant that is upright and vigorous.
Pagoda	Red	M	Deep scarlet red. A deep flower—large, formal double to rose form. Plant is compact.
Professor Tsai	Pink	M–L	Rose pink. Blossoms are medium size, semidouble with undulating petals. Spreading, open growth.
Purple Gown	Red and white	M	Deep purplish red with some white markings. Large flowers are formal double to peony form with wavy petals. Compact plant with very attractive foliage and habit.
Shot Silk	Pink	M	Brilliant pink. Large, loose, semidouble flowers with iridescent, wavy petals. Vigorous, fast-growing plant.
William Hertrich	Red	M	Deep cherry red. Very large blooms are semidouble; outer petals are large and reflexed, smaller inner petals are interspersed with stamens. Vigorous, bushy.

SASANQUAS

Name	Color	Description
Apple Blossom	White and pink	White blushed pink. Single flowers. Growth is vigorous and spreading.
Bonanza	Red	Deep red. The large flowers are a semipeony form. Vigorous, low plant.
Chansonette	Pink	Brilliant pink. Large, formal double with ruffled petals. Spreading growth.
Cleopatra	Pink	Rose pink. Semidouble with narrow, curving petals. Upright, compact, good for hedges.
Dazzler	Red	Brilliant rose red with fairly large, semidouble blossoms.
Hana-Jiman	White and pink	White edged with pink. Large flowers are semidouble with fluted petals. Upright, compact.
Hugh Evans	Pink	Single pink blossoms, free-blooming. Upright, willowy growth; takes sun.
Jean May	Pink	Shell pink. Large, double flowers and upright, compact plant with very glossy leaves.
Mine-No-Yuki	White	White; large, semidouble to peony-form flowers. Spreading, willowy growth. *Synonym:* White Doves.
Momozono-Nishiki	Pink and white	Rose shading to white. Large semidouble with twisted petals. Upright, bushy.
Narumi-Gata	White and pink	White shaded pink; large, cupped single flowers. Compact, upright, and vigorous.
Pink Snow	Pink	Light pink with hint of lavender; large semidouble blooms. Low, spreading plant.
Rainbow	White and red	Large, single white, each petal bordered with red. Plant is bushy and upright.
Setsugekka	White	White; large and semidouble with fluted petals. Upright, bushy growth.
Shinonome	Pink	Soft flesh pink; large, single to semidouble bloom. Plant is upright and bushy.
Shishi-Gashira	Red	Rose red, semidouble to double, medium size blooms over 5-month season. Low, arching growth builds up in time. Can take full sun.
Showa-No-Sakae	Pink	Soft pink, sometimes marbled with white. Medium-large, semidouble to rose form. Fast-growing, willowy, arching habit. Espalier, ground cover, or hanging basket.
Showa Supreme	Pink	Soft pink with large, peony-form flowers. Growth like that of Showa-No-Sakae.
Tanya	Pink	Deep rose pink, single flowers. Spreading, bushy plant—good as ground cover.
Yuletide	Red	Bright red, single flowers with yellow stamens. Dense and upright growth. Blooms in late fall and winter.

HYBRIDS

Name	Color	Season	Description
Anticipation	Pink	M	(Saluenensis-japonica) Deep lavender rose. Flowers are large, full peony form. Upright growth.
Aztec	Red	E–L	(Reticulata-japonica) Deep rose red. Very large, irregular semidouble to loose peony form. Plant is vigorous, upright, open.
Charlean	Pink	M–L	(Japonica-saluenensis) Medium pink with suggestion of orchid. Blooms are large, semidouble on a strong, broadly upright plant.
China Lady	Pink	M	(Reticulata-granthamiana) Rich orchid pink. Very large, irregular semidouble blossoms. Plant is vigorous and upright, with long, narrow leaves.
Coral Delight*	Pink	M	(Saluenensis-japonica) Deep coral pink. Medium-size, semidouble flowers. Growth is slow, bushy, and compact, with small, dark green leaves.
Donation*	Pink	M	(Saluenensis-japonica) Orchid pink. Large, semidouble blooms produced very freely on compact, upright plant. Quite resistant to sun and cold.
Dorothy James	White and pink	M	(Cuspidata-saluenensis-japonica) Petals are white at base, shading to pale pink and edged with rose pink. Medium-size formal double blooms on a slow-growing, compact, upright plant; an excellent container subject.
Dr. Clifford Parks	Red	M	(Reticulata-japonica) Orange-toned, rich red. Blooms are very large, semidouble to peony form or anemone form. Plant is vigorous and upright.
E. G. Waterhouse*	Pink	M–L	(Saluenensis-japonica) Light pink. Medium-size, formal double blossoms are generously produced on a strong, upright plant.
Elsie Jury	Pink	M–L	(Saluenensis-japonica) Medium pink with orchid cast. Large flowers of full peony form on a spreading and somewhat open plant.
Fire Chief*	Red	L	(Japonica-reticulata) Deep but bright red. Large blooms vary from semidouble to peony form. Plant is vigorous, broadly upright, and compact.
Flower Girl	Pink	M	(Sasanqua-reticulata) Bright pink; large to very large, semidouble to peony-form flowers. Vigorous, upright plant with fairly small foliage.
Fragrant Pink	Pink	E–L	(Rusticana-lutchuensis) Deep pink. Fragrant flowers (from C. lutchuensis parent) are miniature, peony form. Growth habit is spreading.
Francie L	Pink	M–L	(Saluenensis-reticulata) Rose pink. Semidouble flowers are very large with high centers and wavy, irregular petals.
Freedom Bell	Red	E–M	Name is suggested by the small, bell-shaped, semidouble blossoms of bright red. Growth is vigorous, upright, and compact.
Harold L. Paige	Red	L	(Japonica-reticulata) Bright red. The blossoms are very large, rose-form double. Plant is strong, with spreading habit.
Howard Asper	Pink	M–L	(Reticulata-japonica) Salmon pink. Blooms are very large, of loose peony form. Large, spreading plant with handsome, large foliage.
J. C. Williams	Pink	E–L	(Saluenensis-japonica) Phlox pink. Medium-size, single, cup-shaped flowers over a long season. Vigorous and upright with somewhat pendulous branches.
Leonard Messel	Pink	M	(Reticulata-saluenensis-japonica) Rose pink. Flowers are large and semidouble, produced on a vigorous, upright, rather open plant.
Miss Tulare	Red	M	(Reticulata-japonica) Bright rose red, the large to very large blossoms varying from rose form to full peony form. Plant is vigorous and upright.
Pink Bouquet	Pink	M	(Japonica-saluenensis) Luminous light rose pink. Semidouble blooms are medium to large, generously produced on a compact, upright plant.
Rose Parade	Pink	E–L	(Saluenensis-japonica) Deep rose pink. Medium-size, formal double blooms appear over a very long period. Vigorous growth is compact and upright.
Terrell Weaver	Red	M	(Reticulata-japonica) Bright to dark red. Large blooms are semidouble to loose peony form with fluted petals. Plant is broadly upright, vigorous.
Valentine Day	Pink	M	(Reticulata-japonica) Salmon pink. Blooms are formal double, large to very large, on a fast-growing, upright plant.
Valley Knudsen	Pink	M–L	(Saluenensis-reticulata) Deep orchid pink. Large to very large blooms vary from semidouble to loose peony form. Strong plant is compact, upright.

Elegans (Chandler)

Elegans (Chandler), Var.

THE ELEGANS FAMILY

Many camellias have originated as mutations (popularly called "sports") on established varieties. The 'Elegans' group is a good example. The original variety was 'Elegans' (Chandler), introduced in 1831. From it developed a variegated sport, and from that came 'C.M. Wilson', which sported to a variegated form and to 'Hawaii'. 'Elegans Splendor', a heavily serrated 'C.M. Wilson' sport, gave rise to 'Elegans Champagne'; 'Elegans Supreme' is a recent sport of the original 'Elegans'.

C.M. Wilson

Hawaii

Elegans Champagne

Elegans Supreme

POPULAR CAMELLIAS OF YESTERDAY AND TODAY

Many of the best-loved and most widely planted camellias have been prized by generations of gardeners. Here is a sampling of such old favorites, including the venerable 'Alba Plena', which in 1792 ushered in the current era of camellia popularity.

Gigantea

Glen 40

Bernice Boddy

Finlandia

Pink Perfection

Ville de Nantes

Alba Plena

ESTABLISHED FAVORITES OF RECENT VINTAGE

Among the countless introductions of the last several decades are some camellias that quickly gained favor, first with specialists and then with the gardening public. Here is a visual sampling of those that show promise of a lasting popularity.

Drama Girl

Guilio Nuccio, Var.

Nuccio's Pearl

Grand Slam

Mrs. D. W. Davis

Tomorrow

Betty Sheffield Supreme

A CAMELLIA POTPOURRI

Varieties of *Camellia japonica* are the most familiar and popular among the general gardening public. But other camellia types are gaining in popularity as their numbers and availability increase. Included among these are varieties of *C. sasanqua*, *C. reticulata*, and diverse hybrids.

Cornelian (C. reticulata)

Tinsie (C. japonica miniature)

Hi-No-Maru (C. japonica, Higo type)

Dr. Clifford Parks (hybrid)

Buddha (C. reticulata)

Momozono-Nishiki (C. sasanqua)

Francie L (hybrid)

China Lady (hybrid)

Chrysanthemum Petal (C. reticulata)

Index

General Subject